The Reality of Christianity: Being a Christian-Believer

BY: LIDA

First published by Dog Ear Publishing
8888 Keystone Crossing
Suite 1300
Indianapolis, IN 46240
www.dogearpublishing.net

ISBN: 978-1457569-967-8
Library of Congress Control Number: 2019938797

This book is printed on acid-free paper.
Printed in the United States of America

I dedicate this book to GOD the Father, the Alpha and Omega of my life. To Jesus Christ, who forgave my sins, delivered me from religious confusion, and gave me salvation. To the Holy Spirit, who gave me my Calling and Gifts of wisdom and knowledge to categorize the three types of religious people: Christlike, Believer, and Christian-Believer. To my husband (Kingsley) who propagates me to Walk N Faith and Not By Sight. To my mother (Katherine), my sister (Valeria), and my brother-n-law (Robert) for encouraging me to Reach for the Stars, No Matter the Starting Point. Lastly, my children (Jonathan, Bianca, Israel, Alexandria, Chibueze, Philip, & Rose) and my niece (Christiana) who all inspire me to Fulfil the Calling on My Life and Operate in the Gifts with the guidance from the Fruit.

Special thanks to Betty, Mark, and Daniel for providing insight and entreating me to give what the Holy Spirit has placed in my spirit.

> **Isaiah 61:1** *The Spirit of the Lord GOD is upon me; because the LORD hath anointed me to preach good tidings unto the meek; HE hath sent me to bind up the brokenhearted, to proclaim liberty to the captives, and the opening of the prison to them that are bound.*

Typos: If there are typos in this book, I apologize it is not my intent to misrepresent any information.

Disclaimer: All Scripture in this book is referenced from the King James Version (KJV), unless identified, minus insertion of any false pseudo books, Apocrypha, originally added due to ignorance, but later removed. This book uses the terms GOD and GODhead interchangeably.

TABLE OF CONTENTS

FIGURES

FAITH N MOTION

What-The-What

Hebrews 11:6 *But without* **Faith** *it is impossible to please HIM: for he that cometh to GOD must believe that He is, and that He is a rewarder of them that diligently seek HIM.* Therefore, is your **Faith N Motion?** And **What-The-What** are you doing by **Faith**?

PART I
INTRODUCTION

KNOWLEDGE FROM THE AUTHOR

Today there are three types of people surrounding Christianity: Christian-Believers, Christlike, and Believers. This book is for Christian-Believers who walk with GOD and believe that Jesus Christ is the second person in the Holy Trinity. There is no doubt concerning a clear line between those who belong to Jesus Christ and those who do not based upon how people view themselves and how their views relate to the world (Wells, 1994, 40). Christian-Believers understand that Jesus Christ is in the Old Testament and in the New Testament. The study of Jesus Christ is called Christology. Christian-Believers should study the WORD of God in order to identify Jesus Christ by HIS Deity (GOD the Son) credentials. The following are foundational Scriptures about the GODhead that all Christian-Believers should know:

    A.   Identification of Jesus Christ separates HIM from all other sources (i.e. gods, persons, animals, etc.).

1. Old Testament References

- ➢ **Genesis**
  - o **3:15** – Christ is born sinless because HE was born of the seed of a woman and not a man. It was the seed of man (i.e. Adam) in **Genesis 3:17**... *cursed is the ground for thy sake.* **Genesis 3:19** ...*for dust thou art and unto dust shalt thou return.* Adam was made from the ground (i.e. dust) therefore; all of his seed are cursed.
- ➢ **Psalms**
  - o **22:1** – Christ's cry at the cross while bearing the sins of the world.
  - o **22:18** – Soldiers cast lots for Christ garment.
  - o **78:2** – Christ would teach in parables.
  - o **118:26** – Christ will be the deliverer.
- ➢ **Isaiah**
  - o **7:14** – A virgin would give birth.
    - ✓ The Hebrew word for virgin is *almah*, which refers to a female that is kept hidden.
  - o **53:5** – Christ would bear the sicknesses of the people.
  - o **61:1** – Christ will be anointed by the Holy Spirit.
- ➢ **Jeremiah**
  - o **31:15** – Herod the King of Judaea killing the children.

- ➤ **Micah**
  - o **5:2** – Coming of the Christ
    - ✓ Christ's birthplace would be Bethlehem.
    - ✓ Christ was here prior to HIS birth on earth.
- ➤ **Zechariah**
  - o **9:9** – Christ would ride as king into Jerusalem on an unbroken animal.
  - o **11:12** – Christ would be sold for thirty pieces of silver.

2. **New Testament References**

- ➤ **Matthew – Apostle Matthew**
  - o **14:33** – Jesus stills the water.
  - o **28:19** – Jesus tells disciples to baptize in the name of the Father, Son, and Holy Ghost.

- ➤ **John – Apostle John**
  - o **1:1–4** – In the beginning was the WORD.
  - o **3:28–31** – John the Baptist recognizes Jesus Christ comes from Heaven.
  - o **6:38** – Jesus bears witness that HE is from Heaven.

- ➤ **Apostle Paul**
  - o **1 Corinthians 1:3–5** – The grace of GOD is given to you by Jesus Christ.
  - o **2 Corinthians 13:14** – The Trinity is identified as GOD,

the Lord Jesus Christ, and Holy Ghost.
- o **Colossians 1:12–17** – Reveals GOD the Father gave HIS Son for deliverance, redemption, and forgiveness.
- o **Hebrews 1:1** – Acknowledges that GOD spake unto the GOD's people through the prophets.

3. **Deity**

  ➢ **Definition of deity:** Essential nature of a GOD

  ➢ **Holy Trinity – GODhead – Systematic Theology**
  - o GOD the Father
    - ✓ The study of GOD the Father is Theology Proper.
    - ✓ GOD the Father's name in Scripture is Yahweh and LORD (all caps).
  - o GOD the Son
    - ✓ The study of Jesus Christ is Christology.
    - ✓ GOD the Son's name in Scripture is Lord, the WORD of GOD, Emmanuel, or Jesus Christ.
  - o GOD the Spirit
    - ✓ The study of GOD the Spirit is Pneumatology.
    - ✓ GOD the Spirit's name in Scripture is the Spirit of GOD, the Holy Ghost, or the Spirit.

- o **Genesis 1:1, 1:25** – Scripture uses the word Elohim – which signifies God unification.

- ➢ **Attributes**
  - o Omnipotent: all-powerful – **Matthew 8:26–27**
  - o Omnipresent: all-present – **John 1:47-50**
  - o Omniscient: all-knowing – **Mark 2:8**

MY TESTIMONY

It was November 1987 when Jesus Christ became real to me. At the age of seventeen, I started my journey of understanding what being a Christian-Believer really entails. The Lord came into my room and asked a question that gave a level of comprehension I had never possessed before. The revelation did not come from the words in the question but rather the underlying meaning the question represented. I was sitting on my bed crying because so many things had gone wrong in my life. The words spoken to me in my room were, "You have tried everything else. Now try me."

The "try me," indicated that Jesus Christ was not impressed by my current loyalty to servitude toward HIM. Those words caused me to deduce the true meaning, which was that I had done everything else in life for fulfillment and none of it was toward Jesus Christ. Although I performed the ritualistic behavior of Christianity and religion, I had never really known or accepted Jesus Christ as my Lord and Savior. The question from the ANGEL of the LORD made me realize that my "works" in the Church and operating in the Gifts were not what the GODhead wanted from me. This event jarred me to remember the Scripture when Jesus Christ said, *Depart from me, ye who work iniquity…* (**Matthew 7:23**).

The realization concerning Jesus Christ's communication with me about my deficiencies in Christianity made me fall to my knees and ask Jesus Christ to show me HIS way. Jesus Christ's way represents complete saturation and implementation of the WORD of GOD into every aspect of life. HIS WAY meant not just attending Church but serving GOD through helping HIS people, dedicating time for holiness (i.e. predetermined time for prayer, fasting, and studying GOD's WORD), and humbling myself to the leadership of GOD's appointed people over my life. That night I made a commitment to surrender my all to HIM.

Before this night, I served GOD by convenience and reservation not seriousness and priority. Prior to this night, I did not mind obeying GOD's WORD as long as it did not interfere with my personal life choices or friendships. In previous times, I would attend Church when there was nothing else to do or while I was at my grandmother's house. Church (i.e. employment of Christianity) was not something I did every day but rather was only on Sundays. I did not attend church out of a sense of necessity or urgency but rather tradition—because Grandma said so. Attending Church was a logical sequence of life applications to fulfill just like Maslow's hierarchy of needs of water and food. I knew I needed to eat food and drink water in order to live, but I was never very particular about what food I ate, and I only drank water when there was nothing else available. I held Church attendance in the same perspective as food. I knew since Grandma was going to Church that I needed to be at Church, but whether the minister taught the undiluted, Holy Spirit filled, anointed WORD of GOD made no difference to me.

After November 1987, I began to love the GODhead with all my heart, my entire mind, all my might, and all my spirit, no matter the consequence. It was after this submission to Jesus Christ that I understood the three deceptions of the enemy within the Church and the Reality of Christianity: Lust of the Flesh, Lust of the Eye, and Pride of Life. Prior to this submission, I had checked all of the boxes of Christianity: praying, fasting, attending Church service, reading my Bible, singing in the choir, and operating in my call and the Holy Spirit gifts. Yet I did not know HIM, Jesus Christ, as my Lord and Savior. My submission to the authority of Jesus Christ helped me to understand the Scripture **Mathew 7:21–23:**

*Not everyone that saith unto me Lord,
Lord, shall enter into the kingdom of
Heaven; but he that doeth the will of
my Father, which is in Heaven. ²² Many
will say to me in that day, Lord, Lord,
have we not prophesied in thy name?
And in thy name have cast out devils?
And in thy name done many wonderful
works? ²³And then will I confess unto
them, I never knew you:* **depart from
me, ye that work iniquity***.*

I thought this Scripture applied to people
who were outside of the Church or hypocrites
within the Church. I had not known it was for
people like me.

Juanita Bynum, while at Azusa, did a
sermon on "The Limp of the Lord." She states:
GOD will use anybody that is available. However,
availability or usage does not mean that the
person or living creature is a Christian-Believer.
GOD uses people who are in the Church for HIS
purpose and/or people outside the Church to
help Christian-Believers. It is written in **Psalms
13:22** *The wealth of the sinner is stored up for
the just.* This availability includes individuals,
animals, insects, and natural disasters to
help GOD's people that serve the Lord Jesus
Christ with a clean heart and a contrite spirit.
A true relationship with Jesus Christ requires

surrendering all. What does the word "all" represent?

It represents dedication and commitment to give all my time, resources, thoughts, and behaviors to serving the Lord Jesus Christ as HE sees fit. This commitment does not come through intellectual exercise but rather dedication to Jesus Christ. This dedication comes in personal prayer time, submission of personal life expectations, and exhibition of behaviors that reflect indoctrination of Scriptures and conduct that brings credit upon Jesus Christ. I am now beginning to understand that peculiar people are Christian-Believers in the twenty-first century. Many people are **PLAYIN' A GAME AND DON'T KNOW THE RULES: The Reality of Christianity.**

I have not always behaved like a true Christian-Believer. My conversion came after the trials and tribulations that would have been easier or nonexistent if Jesus Christ was the pilot and had the wheel to drive me. It is through consequences of disobedience that I suffered hardships and learned the value of obedience with a contrite spirit. I have learned that being a Christian-Believer is not intellectual, physical, social, or emotional. Being a Christian-Believer is a commitment and dedication in your ideas, thoughts, behavior, personality, and lifestyle to a single focus of faithfulness to the WORD of Jesus Christ.

These adjectives are critical in Christianity because of **Proverbs 23:7:** *For as he thinketh in his heart, so is he.* Our thoughts become actions, actions exhibit behaviors, a set of behaviors is a personality type, personality types develop a personality, and it is your personality that is the premise in which lifestyle choices exist. As a child, I always thought of myself as being intelligent. These thoughts led to my actions of taking difficult classes and pursuing higher education.

Taking difficult classes had led to me being in school every year of my life save one year since Kindergarten. Attending school has become part of my personality. I have graduated from high school and earned two associate degrees, two bachelor's degrees, two master's degrees while on active duty in the military, and currently pursuing a doctorate. These accomplishments came because I thought I was smart and acted accordingly.

Comprehension is a prerequisite for Biblical knowledge and wisdom, especially in Christianity. Since comprehension is necessary in Christianity, how can ideologies and enforcement of behaviors that are contrary to Scripture exist in the Church? The Bible clearly teaches in **Galatians 3:28,** *There is neither Jew nor Greek, there is neither bond nor free, there is neither male nor female: for ye are all one in Christ Jesus.* How can a Christian-Believer engage in racism, ethnocentricity, sexism, ageism, etc.? The Prophet writes in **Hosea 4:6,** *My people are destroyed for lack of knowledge: because thou hast rejected knowledge.* The thirteen Original Colonies, which later became the United States, understood oppression when Great Britain oppressed them, but they could not comprehend that they were advocates for oppression.

Native Americans, Africans (i.e. Blacks), Chinese, and other non-Europeans were oppressed by Great Britain and later the United States of America. This oppression came in many forms (genocide, slavery, discrimination, and prejudice). Women also suffered oppression, no matter their ethnicity, in the form of the inferiority stereotype related to intellect, competency, and stamina. This perceived inferiority gave way to societal justification for blocking women in the areas of education, Church leadership, voting, and property ownership. Christian-Believers must *study to show thyself approved until GOD* (**2 Timothy 2:15**). They must pray for revelation knowledge to comprehend the whole Bible in content and context from **Genesis 1:1** through **Revelation 22:21. In Jeremiah 33:3,** the prophet says, *Call unto me, and I will answer thee, and show thee great and mighty things, which thou knowest not.* God lets us know about the inability of man without HIM, and reinforces this within **Romans 7:18:** *For I know that in me (that is, in my flesh,) dwelleth no good thing: for to will is present with me; but how to perform that which is good I find not.* Do not confuse the term man to represent only males; man also represents humankind, we must understand the content and context to distinguish.

PART II
REFLECTION ON STANDARDS

Amos 3:3
Can Two Walk Together, Except They Be Agreed?

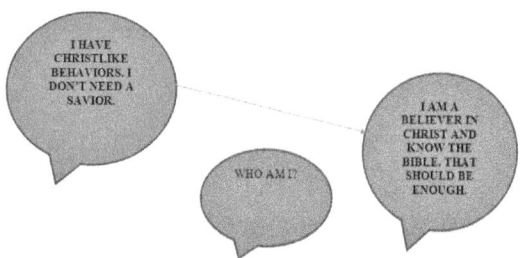

Different ideologies on the authority of life choices and behaviors can give you numerous perspectives on the answers in order to complicate the question. Presumptions appear on the surface to be the same due to use, but their meaning is decidedly different. Therefore, individuals begin a conversation about GOD, Biblical principles, and the Holy Spirit, but their comprehension concerning the vernacular of terms are based upon interpretation of standards, behavior, and life choices that are decidedly different. **People assume where an economy is most efficient it is also most ethical** (Wells, 1994, 8).

CHRISTIAN-BELIEVER

The name "Christian" is being used in a disrespectful manner to ascribe any person or group that shows at least one attribute of Christ. For instance, any individual or church body that acknowledges the name of Jesus Christ irrespective of implementing the attributes of Jesus Christ such as the Son of GOD, Emmanuel, Messiah, Savior of the World, remitter of sins, and gateway to Heaven are of no consideration can be viewed as a Christian or a Christian church. **What-The-What is going on with GOD's people**. This is why the GODhead gave me new names for the twenty-first century Church to identify the peculiar people of the GODhead and distinguish them from those who are not. These triad names for "Christians" are Christian-Believers, Christlikes, and Believers in the world today.

All nectarines are fruit, but not all fruits are nectarines. This dichotomy of fruit and nectarines shapes the similitude between Christian-Believers, Believers, and Christlike persons. What we have today are a small portion of Christians from the New Testament (i.e. Christian-Believers) with a majority being Christlike and Believer people. Christian-Believers put the GODhead first in every area of their life, and "I" is not a common word in their vocabulary.

Is not "I" the vernacular of Lucifer (i.e. Satan, the Devil, and the Dragon)? Isaiah records Lucifer's deceit in 14:12–15: *¹²How art thou fallen from Heaven, O Lucifer, son of the morning! How art thou cut down to the ground, which didst weaken the nations! ¹³ For thou hast said in thine heart, I will ascend into Heaven, I will exalt my throne above the stars of God: I will sit also upon the mount of the congregation, in the sides of the north: ¹⁴ I will ascend above the heights of the clouds; I will be like the MOST HIGH. ¹⁵ Yet thou shalt be brought down to Hell, to the sides of the pit.*

There is no I in team nor pride in salvation. Christlike people think denomination membership, financial contributions, and membership in charitable organizations with save the world strategies are what makes them Christians. Believers are the other antagonist to Christianity. These persons know the GODhead is true and just but choose not to follow. Christlike people and Believers mold their decision-making and lifestyle choices on "I" not Scripture. Christian-Believers know the Scriptures and **follow** the GODhead in every area of their lives.

No matter how a person or group may appear on the surface, without the guidance and leading of the GODhead through the Holy Bible that contains the Old and New Testament, these groups are not part of the family. Do not insult me with a conversation about intertestamental/ pseudo books. Known, accepted, and established leaders of Judaism wrote the Old Testament (Moses, Joshua, Samuel, David, Solomon, Isaiah, Jeremiah, Nehemiah, etc.). Jesus Christ's disciples, later called the apostles, and their immediate disciples wrote the New Testament. The Canonization of the books in the New Testament comes through three authoritarian requirements:

- Authorship is only through Apostolic lineage
- Universality acceptance and usage of the book within the Church.
- Consistent with the Holy Bible concerning GOD, HIS message, and people's redemption.

Apostolic lineage means a book written by a disciple/apostle of Jesus Christ and/or their known apprentice/disciple. The New Testament only has two apprentice/disciples who wrote a book: 1) John Mark, author of the book of Mark, was a disciple of Peter, and 2) Luke, author of the books Luke and Acts, was a disciple of Paul.

The indwelling of the Holy Spirit/Holy Ghost with evidence of speaking in tongues is a cornerstone in Christianity. Speaking in tongues is not a gift but a manifestation of the indwelling of the Holy Spirit in order for the Gifts to flow through. The personal indwelling of the Holy Spirit into the GODhead's people gives them power over the enemy that memorization, motivation, ordination, and good behavior cannot provide. The Holy Spirit tells of the past, present, and future events to the prophet. Is there a prophet in your Church? Are the gifts of healing operating in your Church? Any denomination that does not support the baptism of the Holy Ghost through evidence of speaking in tongues, operation of the five-fold ministry, and the manifestation of the nine spiritual gifts is not part of the GODhead family (i.e. Christianity).

Obtaining one or two attributes of Jesus Christ and using one of the disciples of the New Testament in your denomination does not equate to your religion being a member of Christianity (i.e. Church of Jesus Christ of Latter-day Saints [Mormons]), Jehovah's Witnesses, Unitarians, etc.). Most religions (i.e. Buddhism, Hinduism, Islam [Muslims], Taoism, Wicca, etc.) have Christlike attributes and characteristics, but they do not have a relationship with the GODhead, nor do they have the power of indwelling of the Holy Spirit/Holy Ghost.

> o   Being a "good" person does not qualify a person to be a Christian-Believer but rather Christlike.

    o   Sitting at home, watching television evangelism is not a Christian-Believer attribute but rather Christlike behavior.

Who are Christian-Believers? These are persons who:

(1) Wholeheartedly believe in Jesus Christ and accept the Old and New Testaments as the only pillars of establishment in their faith.

(2) Believe in GOD the Father Almighty, maker of all things in Heaven and in Earth.

(3) Know that Jesus Christ is the only begotten son of the LORD GOD.

(4) Believe that Jesus Christ's conception was a result of the work of the Holy Spirit: that HE was born of a virgin named Mary from the tribe of Judah, suffered under the punishment of Pontius Pilate, was literally crucified, died under the terms of cessation in the senses and operation of breathing, and was buried in a literal tomb.

(5) Comprehend, accept, and are in agreement with the Biblical accounts that Jesus Christ descended into Hell (a literal place), rose from Hell on

the third day; ascended into Heaven (a literal place), and sits at the right hand of GOD the Father.

(6) Commit to, and are in agreement with, the Holy Trinity of GOD the Father, GOD the Son, and GOD the Holy Spirit (i.e. the GODhead).

(7) Believe GOD is the only Creator of all things living and nonliving.

(8) Comprehend, accept, and are in agreement with the deity of the GODhead and that GOD is omnipresent, omniscient, and omnipotent.

These criteria are essential prior to reading and understanding the Bible. The GODhead consists of GOD the Father (i.e. Yahweh and Jehovah), GOD the Son (i.e. Jesus Christ and the WORD of GOD), and the GOD the Spirit (i.e. the Spirit of GOD, the Holy Spirit, and the Holy Ghost).

WHAT DEFINES A CHRISTIAN-BELIEVER

Attributes

- A person who has a personal and intimate relationship with the GODhead (God the Father, God the Son, and God the Spirit).

- A person who exemplifies the teachings of Jesus Christ and upholds the truth of the whole Holy Bible in their behavior and decision-making.

- A person whose values and convictions are the premise for lifestyle choices during times of prosperity, trials, and tribulation.

- Neither intelligence nor academia are the premise for believing, but rather internalized faith in GOD the Father (i.e. Yahweh), Jesus Christ (i.e. the Son of GOD the Father, savior of the whole world, remitter of sins), and the Holy Spirit (i.e. baptism, imparter of spiritual gifts and callings) who are able to protect, guide, and provide salvation. (Do you think slavery, segregation, and sexism are righteous attributes of Christian-Believers?)

- A person who has a true commitment to active participation and relationship in the things for the GODhead in their personal life, professional career, and social environments.

Christianity requires not only outward appearance but also inward transformation in thought and behavior.

Identifiers

Distinguishing Christian-Believers from Christlike Persons and Believers

1. A Believer believes as an intellectual exercise of acknowledgement of Jesus Christ but does not make any changes to lifestyle, behavior, or decision-making. A Christian-Believer follows the whole Holy Bible from Genesis to Revelation (sixty-six books) and obeys all of GOD's written WORD found in the Scriptures.

2. A Believer twists the "Bible" to fit his or her lifestyle choices. A Christian-Believer works to make his or her lifestyle resemble the teachings of the Holy Bible.

3. A Christlike person goes, but is not committed, to the Church of Jesus Christ. They go on holidays, special events, weddings, and funerals. A Christian-Believer knows that their relationship with Jesus Christ is exhibited through obedience in the Household of Faith (i.e. Church community) because it is the paradigm of Christianity.

    *   **1 Corinthians 14:12** *Even so ye, forasmuch as ye are zealous of*

> *spiritual gifts, seek that ye may
> excel to the edifying of the Church.*

4. A Christlike person attends Church
    for someone to serve them and their
    family. A Christian-Believer comes to
    Church to be a servant.

    - **Matthew 23:11** *But he that is
      greatest among you shall be your
      servant.*

5. A Christlike person reads religious
    teachings when things get tough. A
    Christian-Believer reads the Holy Bible
    regularly.

6. A Christlike person prays when things
    get tough. A Christian-Believer gives
    thanks to GOD (i.e. prays) no matter
    the circumstance.

7. A Christlike person will sacrifice when
    it is convenient. A Christian-Believer
    will obey no matter the sacrifice or
    potential outcome.

8. A Christlike person tithes when it is
    convenient. A Christian-Believer will
    tithe a minimum of a tenth of their
    income and pay offering according to
    their abundance.

    - **Deuteronomy 26:2** *Thou shall
      take of the first fruit of all the
      fruit of the earth, which thou shalt
      bring of thy land that the* Lord *thy*
      GOD *giveth thee…*

- Do not insult GOD by thinking that tithes are only for the Old Testament and not the New Testament. IF tithes are only for the Old Testament and not the New Testament, then the blessings and promises from the Old Testament are not for the New Testament.

9. A Christlike person tithes on their net income. A Christian-Believer will tithe on their gross income.

- During the New Testament Christian-Believers paid taxes to Rome, but this did not cause them to delineate from their tithe to the Household of Faith. The fact that a person questions the tithing amount shows their relationship with the GODhead.

Christlike persons are not the New Testament Christians.

- **John 6:64** *But there are some of you that believe not. For Jesus knew from the beginning who they were that believed not, and who should betray HIM.*

    o Jesus was speaking to the disciples traveling with HIM, who either left or betrayed HIM.

Christians

- **Acts 11:26** *And when he had found him, he brought him unto Antioch. And it came to pass, that a whole year they assembled themselves with the Church, and taught much people. And the disciples were called Christians first in Antioch.*

  - **Christians operate according to the Great Commission.**

    - **Matthew 28:19** *Go ye therefore, and teach all nations, baptizing them in the name of the Father, and of the Son, and of the Holy Ghost.*

    - **John 21:17** *HE saith unto him the third time, Simon, son of Jonas, lovest thou me? Peter was grieved because HE said unto him the third time, lovest thou ME? And he said unto HIM, Lord, thou knowest all things; thou knowest that I love thee. Jesus saith unto him, Feed MY sheep.*

    - **Acts 6:2, 4** *Then the twelve called the multitude of the disciples unto them, and said, It is not reason that we should leave the WORD of GOD, and serve tables. ⁴But we will give ourselves continually to prayer, and to the ministry of the WORD.*

- **Acts 20:25** *I have shewed you all things, how that so labouring ye ought to support the weak, and to remember the WORDS of the Lord Jesus, how HE said, It is more blessed to give than to receive."*

Definition of the word Christian:

Verb: to show an outward appearance that is similar to the followers of Jesus Christ in the book of Acts

Not all Believers are Christians.

- **James 2:19** *Thou believest that there is one GOD; thou doest well: the devils also believe, and tremble.*

- **Mark 5:6–9** *But when he saw Jesus afar off, he ran and worshipped HIM, ⁷ And cried with a loud voice, and said, What have I to do with thee, Jesus, thou Son of the MOST HIGH GOD? I adjure thee by GOD, that thou torment me not. ⁸ For HE [Jesus Christ] said unto HIM, Come out of the man, thou unclean spirit. ⁹ And HE [Jesus Christ] asked him [the demons], What is thy name? And he [the demons] answered, saying, My name is Legion: for we are many.*

Definition Of Believer:

Verb: to have confidence in the truth, the existence, or the reliability of something.

Demons believe in GOD and know Jesus Christ as the Son of GOD, but they serve Satan.

- **Acts 13:9–10** *Then Saul, (who also is called Paul,) filled with the Holy Ghost, set his eyes on him. ¹⁰And said [i.e. Paul to the sorcerer], O full of all subtilty and all mischief, thou child of the devil, thou enemy of all righteousness, wilt thou not cease to pervert the right ways of the Lord?*

  o Satan, demons, and their puppets are against everything about GOD the Father, GOD the Son (i.e. Jesus Christ), GOD the Spirit (i.e. the Holy Spirit), and all the people of GOD who serve them.

The Difference

A Believer is familiar with the teachings of the sixty-six books of the Bible but does not comprehend the GODhead or accept Jesus Christ as their Lord and Savior. This person does not practice the teachings in the sixty-six books of the Bible. Believers do not change their lifestyle or decision-making process, nor do they rely on Jesus Christ for protection or take the guidance of the Holy Spirit for direction into their daily lives. Believers may read the book, but they only partially accept the teachings of the Bible. These persons use discretion when it comes to being doers and appliers of the Holy Scriptures. Anyone can be a Believer, but not all who believe are Christian-Believers. **James 2:19** *Thou believest that there is one GOD' thou doest well: the devils also believe, and tremble.* Demons are spirits who serve Satan/Lucifer and who are Believers. The misconception about being a Believer can also merge into the definition of being a Christian.

By the strictest definition, the word "Christian" is the exhibition of an overt behavior interpretation as determinant of being Christlike. To identify a Christian, all one has to do is observe the behavior, lifestyle, or philosophies of said person. This is not the New Testament definition of a Christian. In this observation, the viewer will determine subconsciously or consciously whether the person's overt actions or spoken thoughts make them a Christian. In modern times, people will correlate the term "good person" with being a "Christian." A "good" person can exhibit Christlike behaviors such as charity, loving others, and treating people the way they would want to be treated (i.e. The Golden Rule), but this does not mean that this person believes in the Trinity or in resurrection of the dead during Judgement Day because salvation only comes through Jesus Christ.

Being "good" is not a prerequisite or determinant variable for being a Christian-Believer; otherwise, many biblical heroes are not in the family group. The word "good" is subjective and dependent upon a societal standard and acceptance. For instance, the institution of slavery was an economically sound and viable source of generating revenue, depending upon a person's perspective. At numerous points in the United States of America's history, many "good Christians" supported slavery, colonization, oppression, suffrage, and bondage of "minority" ethnic groups from the White House to the barnyard. These actions placed many ethnic groups into a "sting" of discrimination, harassment, and prejudice. This understanding of "good" creates misleading conceptual models for Christianity and is perpendicular to acceptable practices written in the Bible.

A Christian-Believer, unlike a "good person," has motivations that stem from GOD the Father, GOD the Son, and GOD the Spirit, which is why these persons reason in a particular way and exhibit their beliefs—because they are GOD's peculiar people. **1 Peter 2:9** *But ye are a chosen generation, a royal priesthood, an holy nation, a peculiar people; that ye should shew forth the praises of HIM who hath called you out of darkness into HIS marvelous light.*

There are Christians who refer to the periods of slavery, colonization, oppression, suffrage, and bondage of "minority" groups as the "Good Ole Days." These words—"Good Ole Days"—represent a time that was "good" for a few but not for the majority of others. The "Good Ole Days" is a contradiction to women and ethnic minority groups. The author of this book represents a conflict of the previous ideologies and implementation strategies of the "Good Ole Days." I am an African American female, cyber security analyst professional (i.e. STEM), wife, mother, retiree from the United States Regular Army, scholar with six academic degrees, doctoral student in information assurance, entrepreneur, businesswoman, and property owner. In the "Good Ole Days," the attributes of LIDA were almost nonexistent for African Americans and/or females.

There has always been a separation between the "ruling" and minority groups. Jews and Romans persecuted Christian-Believers from the time of Jesus Christ walking on earth approximately 7 BC until the Edict of Milan (AD 313). This Edict legalized the toleration of the Christian religion under Emperor Constantine over 200 years after the resurrections of Jesus Christ. The Fourteenth Amendment in the United States Constitution gave African Americans citizenship in 1868; the Fifteenth Amendment in 1870 allowed African American males to vote, but it was not until forty-nine years later and the passing of the Nineteenth Amendment in 1919 that women were allowed to vote. The Civil Rights Act of 1964 legally stopped segregation laws in federal, state, and local governments but implementation is another matter.

Women did not gain permission to join the Regular Army officially until 1978 with the deactivation of the Women Army Corps (WAC). As you can see, the "Good Ole Days" were not good days for all of us in the United States. During this time of racism and sexism in the United States, some of the same people who developed and enforced these laws of prejudice were "good Christians" with upright values and regular attendance to the Household of Faith, but I would not call them Christian-Believers (but rather Christlike persons). These Christlike persons do not walk in the conviction that sin is disobedience to the GODhead with the price of Hellfire. They do not comprehend that their innate nature is sinful, and only through the blood of Jesus Christ are sins forgiven, the anointing of the Holy Spirit that gives power over Satan, and only through Jesus Christ is salvation possible. Rather, they only exercise some attributes of the Christian faith. **1 Peter 4:18** *And if the righteous scarcely be saved, where shall the ungodly and the sinner appear?*

DECEPTIONS

Deception 1: Attending Church services regularly can make a person a Christian-Believer in Jesus Christ with a guaranteed ticket for salvation and citizenship in Heaven.

I have always been an active member of a local Church. My mother took my sister and me to our grandmother's house every weekend until I was thirteen years old. My grandmother was a faithful member of a United Methodist Church around the corner from her house. This meant there was no such thing as missing Church. This active participation in Church attendance for the first thirteen years of my life gave me the misunderstanding that I was a Christian-Believer on my way to Heaven because of my actions at Church. I understood this because people at Church would praise me for my efforts and compliment me on how good I was. It never occurred to me that being a Christian-Believer meant sincere commitment and sacrifice to Jesus Christ and the WORD of GOD in my personal life, professional career, and social environment.

Sincere commitment as a Christian-Believer recognizes that personal objectives and life expectations are not significant compared to the mission or ministry of serving the GODhead.

In my delusional state concerning matters about Christianity, I thought Christian-Believers' values were something you did on Sunday and attempted the rest of the week. It was not until I was seventeen, the day the Lord spoke to me, that I realized how wrong I had been. HE said, "You have tried everything else, now try me." This day I understood that what I had been doing since the age of five was Christlike and Believer-focused, I was not a Christian-Believer who followed Jesus Christ.

Reality: Doing church activities with superficial behavior of deliverance and salvation does not make you a Christian-Believer who is Heaven bound.

Deception 2: Active involvement in Church activities and knowing Biblical characters makes you a Christian-Believer with guaranteed salvation.

I thought being a Christian-Believer meant praying, fasting, reading my Bible, going to Church, singing in the choir, paying tithes, and other overt Church activities (i.e. visible participation). These activities, although admirable, do not make you a Christian-Believer. Many people misunderstand this about Christianity. Jesus reinforces HIS displeasure in shallow representation of faith through activities. **Matthew 7:22–23** *Many will say to me in that day, Lord, Lord, have we not prophesied in thy name? And in thy name have cast out devils? And in thy name done many wonderful works?* [23] *then will I profess unto them, I never knew you: depart from me, ye that work iniquity.*

These persons that call on Jesus did many "works," but these activities did not make them a Christian-Believer. The sincerity of actions of a Christina-Believer comes from a relationship with GOD through submission of their will to the will of the GODhead. Jesus Christ, though HE was GOD the Son, submitted to the will of the GODhead. Scriptures shows two submissions by Jesus. **Matthew 4:1** *Then was Jesus led up of the Spirit into the wilderness to be tempted of the devil.* **Luke 22:42** *Father, if thou be willing, remove this cup from me: nevertheless not my will, but thine, be done.* The submission of one's will to the GODhead is a daily process—mentally, spiritually, and physically:

1) Establish and maintain a committed time for personal prayer to the GODhead. Established daily prayer time will allow you to separate and focus toward communication with the GODhead.

2) Commit to a daily or weekly study and meditation of the WORD of

GOD. *"Study to shew thyself approved unto* GOD **2 Timothy 2:15**, so that revelation knowledge may come to your through the GODhead. The Holy Spirit can provide revelation knowledge to you through the GODhead.

3) Lastly, develop an established prayer time that will help you make lifestyle choices that will outwardly and inwardly deliver you from the evil and darkness of our society.

Unlike other religions, "works" in Christianity are not requisites for salvation but rather a repentant heart. **2 Chronicles 7:14** *If my people, which are called by my name, shall **humble** themselves, and **pray**, and **seek my face**, and **turn from their wicked ways**; then will I hear from Heaven, and will forgive their sin, and will heal their land.* It is because of the "traditions" of men (**Colossians 2:8**) who exhibit Christlike behavior on Sunday. Good intentions are nice, but "good" intentions cannot get your sins forgiven. People throughout history had good intentions, but not according to GODhead inspiration or direction. **Proverbs 21:2** *Every way of a man is right in his own eyes: but the LORD pondereth the hearts.*

Throughout my childhood and teenage years, the teaching of Scriptures consisted mainly of Bible stories about Jesus Christ, Moses, Daniel, Jonah, and the other Biblical characters. I thought reciting the sixty-six books of the Bible through a song was sufficient to justify me as a Christian-Believer. When someone would ask me, "Do you know the Bible?" I would say yes because I knew the song. Knowing the books of the Bible is prestigious in the Church. It never occurred to me that Biblical comprehension meant knowing the location, author, teaching, history, and application of Scriptures with chapter and verse. The comprehension of content and context of Biblical truth is not something I remember being enforced at Church, and so I did not consider it relevant or a priority.

Biblical knowledge without the Holy Spirit, content, and context is meaningless because misinterpretation can erupt and deceive many. For instance, we must not use our culture, environment, or inhibition with societal norms when studying Scriptures because doing so will cause unforeseen problems and confusion. This misunderstanding of the content and context will lead you in a direction of confusion and despair. Misdirected motivation based upon misunderstanding happens a lot in Christianity. A person may think Paul wants all Christian-Believers to be a prophet because of what he says in **1 Corinthians 14:1:** *Follow after charity, and desire spiritual gifts, but rather that ye may prophesy,* this is untrue. **A Prophet does prophesy, but the gift of prophecy does not make the Christian-Believer called into the Office of the Prophet.**

The Gift does not equate the office. A prophet is a leadership position (i.e. office) in the body of Christ given by GOD for a specific purpose with permission. We cannot ask to be a prophet; GOD chooses prophets independently of anyone's desires or wishes. **Jeremiah 1:5** *Before I formed thee in the belly I knew thee; and before thou camest forth out of the womb I sanctified thee, and I ordained thee a prophet unto the nations.* The prophet operates in the Gift of Prophecy, but prophets can also operate in the Gift of Revelation, Gift of Knowledge, and the Gift of Wisdom. It was a good effort for people to infer that prophecy represents being a Prophet and Christian-Believers want to be the vessel that hears from GOD to give to GOD's people, but this motivation is not according to knowledge. **Romans 10:2** *For I bear them record that they have a zeal of GOD but not according to knowledge.*

One area of that represents zeal but not according to knowledge is the postulation that the name Jesus Christ in the New Testament is Yehoshua, Jehoshua, Hoshea, Oshea, or Joshua of the Old Testament. The writers of the New Testament Gospels spoke and wrote in Koine Greek (i.e. the language of the people) not Hebrew with the exception of Matthew. Who wrote his first Gospel in Hebrew but no one can read it so wrote another version in Koine Greek (read Eusebius's Church History). This disagreement reveals the lack of comprehension in the content and context of Jesus Christ. The following are reasons why Jesus is not Joshua or Yehoshua in Hebrew:

1. **Definition of the names Jesus, Immanuel, Oshea, and Joshua.**

   a. The prophet Isaiah writes about Immanuel (**Isaiah 7:14**), which the apostle Matthew references Immanuel concerning Jesus Christ in **Matthew 1:23** *Behold, a virgin shall be with child, and shall bring forth a son, and they shall call HIS name Emmanuel, which being interpreted is, GOD with us.* HIS earthly name is Jesus Christ or Jesus the Christ. The name Christ represents the word Messiah, which means *Anointed One;* therefore, by deductive reasoning Jesus must represent the word Immanuel/Emmanuel that means *GOD is with us*.

b. Joshua is not his original name but Oshea. The name Oshea is synonymous with Hoshea, which means salvation. Joshua means GOD saves or GOD helps. Jesus is Immanuel, which means GOD is with us. Which name depicts Jesus's ministry best "GOD saves/helps" or "GOD is with us?" The answer to this question comes from **John 1:1** *In the beginning was the WORD, and the WORD was with GOD, and the WORD was GOD.*

c. The name Hoshea is referenced in the Old Testament to people other than Joshua, in the successor of Moses. The name represents a leader over the tribe of Ephraim (**1 Chronicles 27:20**) and the last leader of the Northern Kingdom (**2 Kings 17:1**). During the time of the Old Testament, it was common to name a son after his father's tribe lineage. Why would GOD name is Son after a rebellious people of Israel who rebuked the blessings of GOD to Judah and David. **Genesis 49:10** *The scepter will not depart from Judah, nor the staff from between his feet, until Shiloh comes and the allegiance of the nations is his.* **2 Samuel 7:16** *And thine house and thy kingdom shall be established forever before thee: thy throne shall be* *established forever*. The fact that the Northern Kingdom formed shows the disobedience of ten tribes hence is why they are called the Lost Tribes of Israel.

2. **The name Joshua is not unique to one person. Which Joshua is the translator referring to as Jesus?**

   a. Joshua is the son of Nun -Tribe of Ephraim (**Numbers 13:8**).

   b. Joshua the Bethshemite– Tribe of Judah (**1 Samuel 6:14, 18**).

   c. Joshua the son of Josedech, a High Priest, – Tribe of Levi (**Haggai 1:14; Zechariah 3:1**).

3. **Name Changes in the Bible**

   a. Abram is renamed Abraham by GOD (**Genesis 17:1**).

   b. Jacob is renamed Israel by GOD (**Genesis 32:28**) but the name Jacob is till used in Scripture to reference a family heritage.

   c. Moses calls Oshea the son of Nun Jehoshua (**Numbers 13:17**), which later is called Joshua.

   d. Nathan calls Solomon Jedidiah because of the LORD (**2 Samuel 12:25**).

   e. Saul is renamed Paul (**Acts 13:9**).

4. **Joshua son of Nun and Jesus come from different tribes**

    a.   Joshua is the son of Nun from the Tribe of Ephraim (**Numbers 13:17**).

    b.   Jesus is from the household of David and David is from the tribe of Judah; therefore, Jesus is from the tribe of Judah (**Matthew 1:1, 2 Samuel 2:4**).

    c.   It was not customary for the Jews during the time of Jesus to name a child that was not part of their family names.

        i.   *When Zechariah's wife Elisabeth was pregnant the ANGEL of the LORD said to call his name John* (**Luke 1:13**), but the people rebuked her for naming a child something that was not his father or tribe. **Luke 1:59-61** *And it came to pass, that on the eighth they came to circumcise the child;* and they *called him Zachariah, after the name of his father. [60] And is mother answered and said, Not so; but he shall be called John. [61] And they said unto her, There is none of thy kindred that is called by this name.*

Reality: Reciting the 66 books in the Bible does not make you a Christian-Believer just a memorizer.

Deception 3: Operating in the Holy Spirit's spiritual gifts guarantees salvation.

At the age of about six years, around the summer of 1976, I saw my first vision. In my vision, I was inside of a department store looking at the doors. I saw in front of the doors, on the inside of the building, two white arc-like panels parallel to each other with enough room for one or two people to walk through. In my dream, it was said to me these machines were alarms to catch criminals. The alarms would go off when a person walked between the two columns in a store with items they did not pay for (i.e. they were stealing). I remember telling my grandmother, "I know how they are going to stop people from stealing from the store, Grandma. They are going to make a machine that will detect stuff that is being stolen from the store when they pass through these things, and an alarm will go off." I told my grandmother about my dream, and she said, "How are they going to detect the stuff?" I said, "With the machines." My grandmother replied to my vision with, "What did you eat last night."

Grandma believed that food has influence on your mood and dreams. I knew what I had seen was not because of what I had eaten. Later on, I understand my dream to be like **Genesis 41:15:** *And Pharaoh said to Joseph; I have dreamed a dream…* Pharaoh has a dream, but he was not a believer in the GOD of the Hebrews. The vision became true in 2003 when I walked inside a department store and saw the machines I seen as a child—inside the store behind a door, just like I had seen at the age of six. By maturing in the GODhead and studying Scripture, I now understand that **having visions or dreams does not make you a Christian-Believer.**

In the summer of 1983, at the age of thirteen, I remember going to my aunt's Lively Stone Pentecostal Church and going up for prayer. Through the movement of the Spirit, I began tarrying for the Holy Spirit; I received my second baptism through full body immersion. I rose from the immersion baptism Speaking In Tongues. From that moment forward, I have prayed through the speaking in tongues and doing the "Holy dance." In my mind, I thought that I had finally committed my life to Christ and was moving forward because I was filled with the Holy Spirit. **With guidance from the GODhead, I began to understand that speaking in tongues, Gifts, and being touched by the Holy Spirit (i.e. the holy dance)**

does not make you a Christian-Believer.
This revelation came because no matter how
many times a day I prayed, until I let go of my
personal agenda and focused on my servitude to
the Lord, the fullness of the GODhead mission
and ministry for my life was not revealed to me.

Reality: Christianity is not a sensation,
systematic, methodological, or intellectual
religion. Rather it is defined by a close and
personal relationship with the GODhead through
Jesus Christ. **John 14:6**...*no man cometh to the
Father but by ME.*

The areas that give the Church the greatest
misunderstanding are:

1. The Bible
2. Biblical Inerrancy
3. Sin
4. Atonement
5. Bodily Resurrection
6. The Untold Story of Job
7. The Holy Spirit
8. The Teacher
9. The Lost Son and Daughter
10. Marks of Maturity
11. The Elect
12. Church Membership

PART III
CHRISTIAN-BELIEVER THEOLOGY

2 Timothy 3:16
All Scripture Is Given By Inspiration Of GOD.

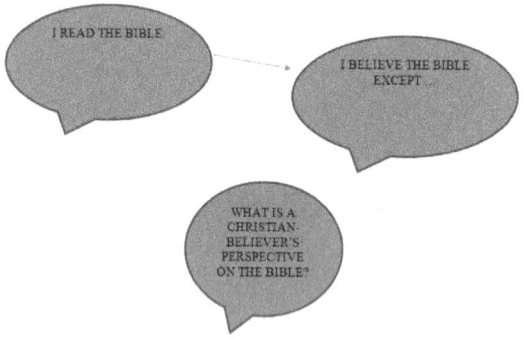

The Bible is either all true or not. A Christian-Believer cannot believe all of the New Testament and not believe all of the Old Testament. GOD is one, and his message is one. GOD is not a man that HE should lie. **Numbers 23:19** GOD *is not a man that HE should lie; neither the son of man that HE should repent: hath HE said, and shall HE not do it? Or hath HE spoken, and shall HE not make it good?*

THE BIBLE

A man enters a restaurant and orders steak and eggs for breakfast. The server returns with his order, and the man is completely baffled at what he sees on his plate. On his plate, the man has eggs that are sunny-side up with a medium-rare steak. The man looks at the server and asks, "What is this?" She replies, "Your order." What is wrong with this situation? The problem is expectation management. The man's presumption for a steak and eggs meal was a well-done steak (i.e. no red showing) and eggs scrambled dry. The server gave him what most customers would have expected upon receiving their order.

People do expectation management every day without knowing it. We elect officials to represent us, and we assume they have Christian-Believer values and convictions to guide their decisions. However, we never actually define what we consider "decisions that have Christian-Believer values and convictions." We PRESUME that politicians hold our Christian-Believer values and convictions because they are "similar" to the laws of the land. This presumption of values and convictions are why many people are surprised when elected officials perform their duties in ways contrary to a Christian-Believer's biblically based values and convictions. Grandma always said, "You can't squeeze blood from a turnip." In other words, if the embodiment of Christian-Believer values and convictions are not the premise for your lifestyle choices, during times of trials and tribulation, these Biblical values and convictions that were once attributes of your character now become options.

Biblical attributes will disappear during times of persecution. Many times, Christlike people will do the "Churchy" thing when they are in trouble, thereby making Christianity an inhibitory response during times of escape until an opening occurs and the real character is revealed. How many times do we see people come to the Household of Faith when their life is at disarray, but the moment things change they run out of the Church and back to confusion? Once the problem dissolves or they gain fame and fortune, individuals return to their excitatory response and forget Christian-Believer's values and convictions. An example of this return is referenced in **Psalms 26:11** *As a dog returneth to his vomit, so a fool returneth to his folly.* Another Scripture cautions against destitution and success in **Proverbs 30:8–9** *Remove far from me vanity and lies: give me neither poverty nor riches;*

feed me with food convenient for me: [9] *Lest I be full, and deny thee, and say, Who is the LORD? Or lest I be poor, and steal, and take the name of my GOD in vain.*

BLUF (Bottom Line Up Front), in order to have a conversation about Biblical truths, all parties (the Christian-Believer, Christlike, and/or Believer) must establish presumptions and agree on Bible doctrinal terms without presumptions based upon word choice. The premise of this conversation between parties requires an understanding of the fundamentals of the Holy Bible using a literal translation. King James Version [KJV] is an example of a literal translation, as opposed to a dynamic translation such as New International Version [NIV] or paraphrase such as the Message [MSG]). KJV is the theological standard by which other English versions are developed. The King James Version, in my choice for scholarly and practical assessment, is the version that holds theological legitimacy, leadership oversight, and legal authority to provide checks and balances. The KJV was ordered by King James I to develop a Bible that was the most accurate. In 1604, James appointed 54 advisors to research the Scriptures. They were organized into six companies, two each working separately at Westminster, Oxford, and Cambridge on sections of the Bible assigned to them. Richard Bancroft (1544–1610), archbishop of Canterbury, served as overseer and established doctrinal conventions for the translators (Britannica, 2019).

These advisors were established theologians in the Christian faith, with oversight of their work by an ordained Archbishop, with the legal backing of the King of England as the authority to bring punishment upon anyone who intentionally misleads or erroneously translates the manuscript (i.e. Scripture) in order to deceive the reader. To my knowledge, no other version has this level of legitimacy, oversight, and authority checks and balances. Have you checked the credentials of the authors of the version or type of Bible that you conduct your Biblical learning and use for authority over your life? Do the authors of these other versions and types of Bibles have a Master of Divinity from an accredited seminary? Yes, this means are the authors of the version you are reading seminary-trained, learned in Bible not counseling and discipleship, and going to an accredited school to learn Bible. There is nothing wrong with specialties in Christianity in seminary but when the specialist lacks comprehension of the Bible in content and context, there is a problem.

There is a large distinction between people

doing full-time ministry and being a Biblical translator of Greek and Hebrew comprehending content and context of Scriptures. The disciples of Jesus were not scholars of the faith with the exception of Paul, but they all knew the Law and were known in their community for being faithful to the Law. Notice no one ever identifies Jesus's disciples as hypocrites; they only called them unlearned, meaning not school-trained (**Acts 4:13**), Andrew – the brother of Peter and John – the brother of James the Elder, were disciples of John the Baptist, but no one calls Paul unlearned or an hypocrite because he was an established and ordained as Pharisee.

Pharisees were the Law keepers during the time of Jesus, who were educated in the Law and could read, write, spell, and articulate in Hebrew. GOD can call anyone to go into ministry, although seminary is a viable option for individuals who consider education a priority. It never ceases to amaze me how Christian-Believers want their physician, attorney, dentist, veterinarians, and public school teachers to be board-certified, which requires being a graduate from an accredited school for the specific field, but anyone that can quote two Scriptures and say amen can be an apostle, prophet, evangelist pastor, teacher, or a bishop in GOD's Church. Please try not to misunderstand the previous statements with singleness of thought. I am not saying everyone in the five-fold ministry or its helpers should be seminary-trained, but if these persons require education for other professional fields (doctors, lawyers, dentists, veterinarians, etc.), why should leaders in the Church be any different.

Those occupations are temporal and containerized for this world, why does not persons who are preparing GOD's people for a fulfilled life with the GODhead through atonement and salvation in this world and everlasting life in the next have not a similar standard of authenticity and professionalism? There are degrees (i.e. Accredited Seminaries) that offer in-depth knowledge for Biblical Studies (learning Greek and Hebrew), Pastoral Counseling (focus-based or objective oriented styles), Chaplains (hospital and military), Christian Historian, Discipleship, Missions, Church Growth, and many others. Does not GOD deserve our best, if you consider higher education pivotal in the improvement of learning, why should Christian Education be any different? Do you have a college degree or encourage others to have one? Why then do we accept others that do not have a degree and want to teach or preach the most important thing to learn in life, GOD the Father, Jesus

Christ the Son, and the Holy Spirit? I have a degree in Theology and Divinity not for the reasons of opening a Church but because I am a Christian-Believer and I want to know all I can about my GOD and grow in the faith of Jesus Christ. **Romans 10:17** *So then faith cometh by hearing and hearing by the WORD of GOD.*

The author's choice for Biblical version is a literal translation using the King James Version (KJV). Why is a literal translation the author's preference? Are not all versions of the Bible the same? The answer to the question is no. A literal translation of the Bible equates to identifying each word in a sentence and placing value on word choice. A dynamic version (NIV) of the Holy Bible fluctuates between literal and paraphrase without giving the reader any warning when translation changes in the text from literal to paraphrase or vice versa.

I don't like when someone is talking to me and they are telling a half-joke and half-reality because I can not distinguish one from the other throughout the conversation. Keep it real or keep it fantasy. A paraphrase version (i.e. Message) of the Bible is application-based only without a literal meaning. Do you want application before you know definition? This type of learning opens the door for confusion and misinterpretation. Selecting a version of the Bible (i.e. literal, dynamic, or paraphrase) may appear to be splitting hairs but it is not. Following is an example of distinction in diction and vocabulary between KJV, NIV, and MSG Bible versions in **Luke 1:27**

- *to a virgin **espoused** to a man whose name was Joseph, of the house of David; and the virgin's name was Mary* (KJV)

- *to a virgin **pledged to be married** to a man named Joseph, a descendant of David.* The virgin's name was Mary* (NIV)

- *to a virgin **engaged to be married** to a man descended from David.* His name was Joseph, and the virgin's name, Mary* (MSG).

This declaration to Joseph being from the house of David in Matthew weighs on the fact of Jesus Christ having kingship lineage, but Mary also is a descendant of David through Nathan in the Gospel of Luke. Matthew's Gospel (**Matt 1:1–16**) reveals Joseph as a descendant from Solomon's lineage giving him kingship ties, and Luke's Gospel (**Luke 3:23-31**) shows Mary as a descendant from Nathan's lineage, while both of Jesus Christ's earthly parents are from Bathsheba. Therefore, Jesus was a descendant of David legally through HIS earthly father (Joseph) and genetically through HIS mother (Mary). The identification of Mary as a descendant of David substantiates why GOD chose Mary to be the only earthly woman to have an Immaculate Conception from the Holy Spirit.

Mary is not special apart from GOD using her womb to bring the Messiah into the world. She was born just like all other women in the world through the seed of a man. Mary gave birth to the Messiah, Jesus Christ. Notice in the KJV, the literal calls Mary *espoused* to Joseph, which during this time meant they were already married, just awaiting ceremony, and only divorce could dissolve the marriage. We know this depiction of already married exists and is accurate from **Matthew 1:19**

- *Then Joseph her husband, being a just man, and not willing to make her a public example, was minded to put her away [divorce] privily* (KJV).

- *Because Joseph her husband was faithful to the law, and yet did not want to expose her to public disgrace, he had in mind to divorce her quietly* (NIV).

- *Joseph, chagrined but noble, determined to take care of things quietly so Mary would not be disgraced* (MSG).

Notice **Matthew 1:19** in the KJV explains Joseph is a *just man* (**Proverbs 24:16** represents a just man as one that is perpendicular to a wicked man). In **Matthew 1:19,** the NIV writes Joseph as faithful to the law, which is what Pharisees, priests, and scribes were supposed to be. **Matthew 23:2-3** *The scribes and the Pharisees sit in Moses' seat:* [3] *All therefore whatsoever they bid you observe, that observe and do; but do not ye after their works: for they say, and do not.* **Matthew 1:19** in the MSG writes Joseph as being *noble.* The world noble is referenced in **Ruth 3:11** *and now, my daughter, don't be afraid. I will do for you all you ask. All the people of my town know that you are a woman of noble character.*

By no stretch of the imagination is Ruth's character synonymous with that of Joseph. Ruth is a Moabite, whose descendants come from an incestual union between Lot and his older daughter (see **Genesis 19:37**), while Joseph is a descendant of David from the line of Jesse, whose father is Obed. Ruth, the Moabite (**Ruth 1:22**), is Obed's wife's. Obed's family line is part of the chosen people of GOD. Obed and Ruth have a son named Jesse, and it is through Jesse's son, David, whom GOD chose to be the King of Israel and unite the tribes of Israel. It is David descendants in line for the kingship of Israel will remain until the judgement day.

Joseph also contemplated divorcing Mary, according to the KJV, by "putting her away privily," which represents that they were legally bound to each other. The NIV version says, "Joseph was faithful to the law," which would have required Joseph to have Mary stoned to death (see **Leviticus 20:10** *And the man that committeth adultery with another man's wife, even he that committeth adultery with his neighbour's wife, the adulterer and the adulteress shall surely be put to death*). How can Joseph be faithful to the Law and not bring justice to the adulterer and the adulteress because Mary was legally espoused to him? **Matthew 1:19** in MSG explains Joseph as going to "take care of things." What things is this version referring to? This interpretation leaves the reader to have gaps in comprehension concerning what the author means and may not understand that Joseph is considering divorcing Mary. This is an example up close and personal between literal, dynamic, and paraphrase.

BIBLICAL INERRANCY

What is the meaning of the term *Bible inerrancy,* and how does it relate to the Bible? The word *inerrant* means "without error." I understand that in a humanistic society people recite words such as, "Your truth is not my truth," but the Bible is hard to grasp. Many people hear the **fanciful** words, "You can be anything you want to be," but it is not true. My favorite person in the Bible is Moses, the author of Genesis, Exodus, Leviticus, Numbers, and Deuteronomy. I admire Moses's faith walk, but no matter how I try to emulate his faith walk or commit my ways to the servitude to the GODhead, I will never be Moses, nor does GOD want me to be. Moses is from the Hebrew lineage of Isaac, Jacob, and Levi. GOD used him to perform miracles that defied science and logic, and he established a theocracy for the Children of Israel.

Speaking words of action, no matter how loud or how many times, will not make those words come true without the mercy and grace of the GODhead. I am 4 feet 11 inches tall. No matter how much I may say I am 6 feet 1 inch tall, I will not grow taller. The Bible defies human reason because it is not based upon human intellect or interpretation of truth.

The GODhead does not need validation from anyone or anything; they are just and holy all by themselves. A Christian-Believer's attitude toward classical pagan ideologies requires including philosophers such as Plato, Aristotle, and the Stoics because to accept them could be a concession to paganism and inroads of idolatry into the Church (Gonzalez, 1984, 53).

Biblical inerrancy represents that the Bible is truth, without error or omission of the original manuscripts. The GODhead breathed HIS WORD, and Biblical authors translated them into their language. The topics surrounding inerrancy of the Bible has been a debate in theological arenas between Christian-Believers, Non-Christians, and Non-Believers alike for years. This debate represents the indecisiveness of man trying to substantiate behavior or validate reasoning apart from GOD's WORD. The Bible is either 100% complete and accurate, or its not; "lukewarm" does not exist. (**Revelation 3:16**) *So then because thou art lukewarm, and neither cold or hot, I will spue thee out of my mouth.* GOD does not want lukewarm, indecisive people; HE wants a people that will obey HIS WORD and serve HIM as their only GODhead. (**Exodus 19:5**) *Now therefore, if ye will obey my voice indeed, and keep my covenant, then ye shall be a peculiar treasure unto me above all people: for all the earth is mine.*

As Christian-Believers, comprehension of the Holy Bible is not a prerequisite for acceptance of Biblical inerrancy, but rather it is an addition. The Christian-Believer must believe because, according to **Hebrews 11:6** *But without faith it is impossible to please HIM: for HE that cometh to* GOD *must believe that HE is, and that HE is a rewarder of them that diligently seek HIM*. Either believe the whole Bible is true, or believe none of the Bible. Let us first consider why the Holy Christian Bible, with its sixty-six books, is true. The word *truth* is non-negotiable. "If the Bible is unable to produce a sound doctrine of Scripture, then it is thus incapable of producing, with any degree of believability or creditability, a doctrine about any other matter" (MacArthur, 1982, 12).

Truth questions are binary with either yes or no answers—maybe is not an option. GOD is not a man that HE should lie (**Numbers 23:19**). HE is not a politician requiring votes to win an election, nor does HE get power from the amount of people who believe in HIM. No matter the questions or answers, GOD is independent of man's scrutiny, opinion, interpretation, or justice to validate or substantiate HIS deity or decisions. When GOD makes a decision, it is just and final without being subject to interpretation or investigation. Due to GOD's love for HIS people, HE may alter

HIS decision because of prayer of the righteous. (**James 5:16**) *...The effectual fervent prayer of a righteous man availeth much.* Whether we like GOD's decision has no influence because GOD is the great I AM. (**Exodus 3:14**) *And God said unto Moses, I AM THAT I AM.* The preacher's job is "to preach the mind of GOD as he finds it in the inerrant WORD of GOD" (MacArthur 1982, 14). Obedience to GOD's WORD is highly suggested because GOD will not force you into obedience nor demand your servitude, but the penalty of disobedience is fierce. It is written in **1 Samuel 15:22:** *And Samuel said, Hath the Lord as great delight in burnt offering and sacrifices, as in obeying the voice of the Lord. Behold, to obey is better than sacrifice, and to harken than the fat of rams.* Comprehension is not a requisite for compliance to GOD's WORD.

The premise of Scripture is to inform the reader that the Bible is the basis for all the teaching, learning, and preaching that the Church needs. There are leaders in the Church to assist with the teaching, learning, and preaching, but in the absence of leadership, the Bible is still available. It is written in **2 Timothy 4:2** *Preach the WORD; be instant in season, out of season; reprove, rebuke, exhort with all longsuffering and doctrine.* This verse describes the steadfastness of Scripture to defeat any doctrine or ideology that opposes the truth. MacArthur answers the questions about the preacher's responsibility. The preacher (i.e. apostle, prophet, evangelist, pastor, or teacher) needs to realize that it is GOD's WORD is "not" the preacher's word. He or she is only the messenger not the originator; sower not the source; herald not the authority; steward not the owner: guide not the author; server of spiritual food not the chef (MacArthur, 1982, 7).

Presumptions

The first clarification of understanding the Old and New Testament is to understand the people and their background. The Hebrews, Israelites, and Jews all come from an oriental background (i.e. where the sun rises, Eastern Religion) not an occidental background (i.e. where the sun falls, Western Religions). Christian-Believers need to understand that the terms *Hebrew, Israelite,* and *Jew* are not synonymous. These terms require comprehension when reading the Old and New Testament. ALL of the children of Abraham are Hebrews. This includes Abraham brother Hebron son Lot, Laban (i.e. Rebecca's brother), Ishmael, Isaac, and his second wife Ketuvah's children. However, not all Hebrew are Israelites. The Israelites come only from the line of Jacob, who is Isaac's son, and Isaac is Abraham and Sarah's son. Not all Israelites are the chosen (i.e. peculiar) people. The peculiar people in Exodus are the people that left out of Egypt with Moses and made a commitment to GOD at Mount Sinai.

The Scripture reads in **Exodus 19:5** *Now, therefore, if ye will obey my voice indeed, and keep my covenant, then ye shall be a peculiar treasure unto me above all people: for all the earth is mine,* for GOD's people have commitment requirements not DNA leniency. The peculiar people in I Peter are Christian-Believers. (**I Peter 2:9**) *But ye are a chosen generation, a royal priesthood, and holy nation, a peculiar people; that ye should shew forth the praises of HIM who hath called you out of darkness into HIS marvelous light.* When we see the term "Jews" arise in the Old and New Testament, it is a derivative of the larger tribe of Judah after the divide. Remember when the twelve tribes separated; 10 tribes were the Northern Tribe, and Judah/Benjamin were the Southern Kingdom (Judah).

The separation of the tribes did not change GOD's declarations. GOD used Jacob (i.e. Israel) to bless Judah. (**Genesis 14:9**) *The scepter shall not depart from Judah, nor a lawgiver from between his feet, until Shiloh come; and unto him shall the gathering of the people be.* GOD gave a promise to David in **2 Samuel 7:16** *And thine* *house and thy kingdom shall be established for ever before thee: thy throne shall be established forever*. Judah is the root word of Judaism. The name "Jew" represents the people during and after the Babylonian and Persian captivity.

Moses records GOD's WORD in the first five books of the Bible, which are the first written Scriptures. The main idea of these Scriptures is found in **Exodus 19:5 *IF YE OBEY and KEEP*... *THEN Ye shall be ABOVE ALL PEOPLE.***

Thus, this clarifies that DNA is not enough to be part of GOD's peculiar people. The gentile nation through adoption and acceptance of **Exodus 19:5** has the inheritance of GOD's peculiar people. Yes, this represents that the Old Testament's calls for obedience are compulsory for the New Testament Church. The New Testament is a continuation of the Old Testament with the acceptance of Jesus Christ as their Lord and Savior. **John 14:6** *Jesus saith unto him, I am the way, the truth, and the life: no man cometh unto the Father, but by me.*

Selective Obedience

The Bible must be inerrant in order for the Bible to have legitimacy. Without inerrancy, the Christian-Believer's Faith is just another set of good ideas or prescribed religious behaviors. When Christian-Believers operate under "selective obedience" to Scripture, this nullifies all the Scriptures of the Holy Bible. We cannot accept the New Testament and denounce the Old Testament. The Bible is one, and its message is one. Hebrews, who are part of the promise in the Abraham-Isaac-Jacob patriarch and faithful to GOD's WORD, are HIS chosen people not by DNA but rather faith and obedience. GOD chose this people to represent HIM on earth. However, they are not the only representatives of GOD on earth because most Hebrews reject Jesus Christ as the Messiah. One of the purposes of anointing the Gentiles is to cause the Hebrews to be jealous and turn back to HIM with understanding of Jesus Christ as the fulfillment of prophecy (**Romans 11:11–14**).

Selective obedience comes about especially in relationships. When we believe **John 3:16** *For GOD so loved the world that HE gave HIS only begotten…*, we must also believe **Galatians 6:7** *Be not deceived, GOD is not mocked: for whatsoever a man soweth, that shall he also reap.* Both of these Scriptures are representations of GOD and are equal in value. Yes, GOD does love you; however; this love does not prevent HIM from enforcing HIS WORD. Christlike people and Believers are especially discretionary with the books/epistles written by the Apostle Paul. Consider **Galatians 3:28** *There is neither Jew nor*

Greek, male or female, bound or free but all are one in Christ Jesus.

People would say Paul is hearing from GOD. This **Scripture** is also true from **Ephesians 5:25** *Husbands, love your wife as Christ loved the Church.* This means husbands are to give unto their wives as Christ did for the Church. People are in agreement with Paul and quote this Scripture frequently with Amen and Hallelujah. But when it comes to the Scripture in **Ephesians 5:22** *Wives submit until your own husbands, as unto the Lord,* people are in disagreement because submission is definitive and is not optional or dependent upon how you feel or like it. A misunderstanding of Scripture can cause a Church to miss blessings from the GODhead.

Paul's writing in **1 Timothy 2:11–12** *Let the woman learn in silence with all subjection.* [12] *But I suffer not a woman to teach, nor to usurp authority over the man, but to be in silence for it is not permitted for a woman to speak.* Question arises about the authenticity of the Scripture. The author of Galatians and Ephesians is the same author of **1 and 2 Timothy**. The message is clear and comes from the same Holy Spirit. Is GOD the author of confusion? Instead of dismissing, research these Scriptures because there is a meaning and purpose. GOD is not the author of confusion.

People will have debates about **1 Timothy 2:11–12**, concerning the oppression of women. This statement of oppression is contrary to **John 3:16** *For GOD so loved the world that HE gave HIS only begotten Son, that whosoever believeth in HIM should not perish, but have everlasting life.* Why would GOD oppress the people that HE loves? Did not GOD inspire all Scripture? GOD uses women in the Bible, Church, and in ministry for leadership positions. Are women the primary or alternate choice to leadership positions? Does it matter? GOD selects individuals based upon HIS criteria. GOD decides whom HE will choose, when HE chooses, and where HE chooses. It is not debatable.

This is made known in **Romans 9:15–16** *For HE saith to Moses, I will have mercy on whom I will have mercy, and I will have compassion on whom I will have compassion.*[16] *So then it is not of him that willeth, nor of him that runneth, but of GOD that sheweth mercy.* Just because you are woman or a man does not mean you are a leader or a follower. GOD will choose whom HE wills when HE desires, for it is written in **I Corinthians 12:11** *But all these worketh that one and the selfsame Spirit, dividing to every man severally as HE will,* because *the gifts and callings of GOD are without repentance* (**Romans 11:29**). The word "man" in this Scripture is not sex-specific but rather means an individual;

remember when reading Scripture consider the content and context.

When Paul is talking about a relationship, the word man refers to the male in a married couple (i.e. *let not the woman teach or usurp authority over the man* [**1 Timothy 2:12**]). The operative words are *content* and *context*. Paul is addressing a particular issue about married couples' relationship and wives not embarrassing their husbands in public. Let us not get caught up in identity crises and gender neutrality; focus on the Scripture because the GODhead does not judge you by your sex. Again, *There is neither Jew nor Greek, there is neither bond nor free, there is neither male nor female: for ye are all one in Christ Jesus* (**Galatians 3:28**).

Selective obedience does not have a place in a Christian-Believer's life or in a body of Christian-Believers' Church. The acceptance of Biblical inerrancy postulates the premise for which a Christian-Believer exists. For a Christian-Believer, the Bible can only be ALL knowledge and wisdom in acceptance, faith, and obedience or not at all. GOD does things in completeness not parts. When people don't accept the WHOLE Bible they are not Christian-Believers but rather Christlike or Believers and just **PLAYIN A GAME AND DON'T KNOW THE RULES: The Reality of Christianity.**

SIN

Postmodernism is man's way of trying to remove the accountability of sinful behavior. There is a distinction between modernization and modernism. One ideology produces changes in the fabric of life; the other alters values and meanings that come from the context of a modernized world (Wells, 1994, 7). Sin is a problem because its nature is perpendicular to the character and authority of GOD. Sin is "failing to acknowledge GOD as GOD" (Erickson, 1998, 579). Throughout history, GOD's creation tries to covet HIS position as GOD. This covetousness is where sin enters and remains. Another problem with sin is how we define sin and what equates to sin. Sin is not a matter of right and wrong but of righteousness versus unrighteousness and obedience versus disobedience.

Things that people accept or tolerate are good and bad depend upon the era or perspective, but this is not GOD's law. The adjective "good" is subjective and therefore is not able to have objectivity or accuracy. Objective means it is true no matter the circumstance. The Bible is an example of objectivity because the rules do not change. The good behavior pendulum sways from left to right depending on the circumstance, country, and culture. In countries that practice Sharia Law, if a man steals, he can face corporal punishment (i.e. removal of hand); however, in the United States the punishment for stealing is negotiable depending on the value of the item stolen. A different perspective on the seriousness of the offense results in different perspectives on the manner of persecution.

Lastly, sin is a problem because of consequences. People can cover their guilt through external means—alcohol, cocaine, smoking, people, exercise, and career—but they cannot cover what GOD put in his WORD for doing such things. In their final attempt to avoid consequences, the denial of sin now exits. This belief is an assumption that sin only applies to certain people. This is the postmodern ideology of everything being relative.

Biblically based sin "speaks of breaking the laws of GOD, either by knowledge or accident" (Hindson & Caner, 2008, 451), it does not matter which law of GOD you break. It is not only the act of wrongdoing but a state of alienation from God (Elwell, 2001, 1103). One Scripture that highlights man's involvement with sin is **James 1:14** *But every man is tempted, when he is drawn away of his own lust, and enticed.* These definitions suggest that sin began before the creation of man because the Prophet

Isaiah writes about Lucifer conniving for the authority of GOD. **Isaiah 14:14** *I will ascend above the heights of the clouds; I will be like the most High.* The angel Lucifer was the first to act in covetousness and seek to have GOD's power and position of authority. Lucifer (i.e. Satan, the Devil, and the Dragon) and one-third of the angels (i.e. demons) in Heaven came up against GOD, which caused their removal from Heaven. These fallen angels' names and positions in Heaven with GOD are changed forever. The initiation of disobedience (i.e. sin) began in Heaven with the fall of Lucifer and he has ushered this disobedience into the earth.

Adam did not create sin; rather, it was because of his and Eve's covetousness that sin is with all humanity. What did Satan use to lure Eve into sin, covetousness? Satan told Eve that she could be a god like GOD and that GOD knew it. What was Satan feeding on? Satan fed on Eve's desire to want to be a god. It was not enough that she had all her needs met in the garden, that she had constant communication with GOD. Why was being godlike so desirable? What is it about knowing something or someone greater than you that persuades a person to believe the only way to gain notoriety is to achieve the same by any means necessary? Men's cupidity is as insatiable as the grave

(Jameison, Fausset, & Brown, 1961, 472). The quote is a commentary from the Scripture **Proverbs 27:20** *Hell and destruction are never full; so the eyes of man are never satisfied.*

Isaiah spoke of this mentality concerning Lucifer. Lucifer decided to make himself equal to GOD by first placing himself in a god mentality. It was only at that point that was he able to contemplate being above GOD —the idea that there are no established boundaries, no absolutes, that everything is relative. This allows someone to want to be GOD (the Almighty, omnipotent, omnipresent, all knowing being) or be a god unto himself. The person will set the standard of right and wrong behavior (i.e. goodness). Their definition of goodness allows the obligation to obey God to be invalid because HE is no longer their god. This means, in their mind, that God no longer has authority over them. These persons think GOD has no authority over them; therefore, sin is now a matter of opinion or perspective.

Perspective

How you perceive sin will determine your perspective on sin. Differing perspectives on sin is the door where postmodernism enters and uses this "hole" to cause confusion among Christians. The questioning of the Christian faith being absolute is substantial considering the number of contemporary New Testament scholars that operate out of the reader-response and postmodern matrices (Carson & Moo 2005, 66). The reader-response theory is dependent on the interpretation of the reader, not the author, or the text. This theory assumes that the reader's understanding of the Scripture is most important; however, this creates a problem when two or more readers many not interpret the same way. In reader-response, they both are correct.

During the first three centuries of the Christian era, the Roman worldview of religions was pluralistic, and the consensus was that there was no one way to GOD. On this perspective by the Romans was a strong agreement on "an axiom of Greek culture that the cosmos was total (including all the gods), perfect and changeless. In times past there was a misunderstanding that human error could be corrected by education" (Carson & Moo, 2005, 34). Education, according to the Greeks, is the key to a sinless life for humans. This theory implies increased education will delete the need for a Savior, thereby nullifying the consequences of sin. This is the same belief held by the Gnostics that "knowledge was superior to faith, and certain enlightened Christians had a special knowledge of the truth" (Lea & Black, 2003, 52).

Another error in Christian history comes from Arminian and Calvinist theology. Arminian thought came from Jacobus Arminius. This theology during the seventeenth century was in opposition to Calvinism from John Calvin. The Arminian ideology supports the doctrine of free will and not predetermination / predestination (i.e. Calvinism). The Arminian belief shows clear lines of misunderstanding of GOD and sin. GOD has a plan for everyone's life; however, this is not predetermination but purpose. Arminian ideology dissolves purpose but rather supports individual choice is the source of your life success and failure. In the Arminian comprehension, everyone is born with a clean slate and this understanding is against Scripture because GOD tells his people numerous times in Scripture I knew you in your mother's womb (i.e. John the Baptist and Jeremiah the Prophet).

Calvinism supports predestination, which dissolves any ones active involvement with their individual choices in life, this understanding is also erroneous. GOD wants us to walk according to HIS will and HIS way according to HIS WORD, Calling, and Gifts upon our life. This will of GOD is unchanged because *the Gifts and Callings of GOD are without repentance* (**Romans 11:29**) but GOD will not force you to be obedient and submissive, it is your choice. Know that disobedience to GOD's purpose for our lives concerning GOD's will is sin. Many people die without every fulfilling the Gifts and Calling on their life by GOD and must give an account of their negligence and disobedience at death and during Judgement Day.

There were many types of council throughout the history of Christian theology to make decisions on Christian matters. The Council of Trent (1545–1563) had the task of clarifying Original Sin. The council makes it clear concerning the usurpation of humans concerning Adam and sin to all humankind. The Council of Trent decided that anyone who did not accept Original Sin was to be detested or accursed to damnation.

Atheists see human creation as a chemistry experiment. Humans were not created; they just happened (Rainer, 2005, 75). Atheists believe humans are a product of evolution, which has no goal or future, just randomness. To the atheist, no one species is more important than any other species; they just have different areas of responsibilities. Plato's Laws X (c.352–380 BC) defined an atheist as moral and upright (McDowell & Stewart, 1983, 414). This view supports that being morally good is an acceptable way of living. Unfortunately, morals and values are subjective with a premise that is derived from an individual, society, or culture. What is morally good in China may not be in Canada—which is one is correct?

Postmodernism uses these perspectives to make different religious views all hold the same value, thereby causing not one view to be the absolute in truth. The reader-response view places the perception of sin on the interpretation of the reader. If the environment in which the reader lives accepts certain behaviors as morally correct, then the sin or behavior is done through ignorance. The correction of the sin would be through education, and the lack of education would lead to consequences until the person educates himself. In a Christian view, due to Adam's disobedience, all humans commit sin not because of education but rather genetics. To the Christian-Believer, sin has consequences that not only affect your physical body but also your soul.

Consequence

Satan was jealous of the high destiny reserved for humankind, and for that reason, he led Adam and Eve into sin. Once Satan's jealous rage was unfolded, the mark of sin unfolded (Gonzalez, 1984, 70). Sin is the consequence of disobedience not the cause of it. Postmodernism uses the rejection of absolute truth to reject addressing the consequences of sin. For postmodernism, everything is relative, thereby not making any one idea greater than the other does. This mindset has wreaked havoc on American society. The notion that things are relative has caused many to question the roles and responsibilities of husband and wife, parents, children, government, and society. In relation to the current thought of many Christlike people, the following scenarios would substantiate a vote for an abortion:

1. A minister and his wife, who live in extremely modest conditions, discover they are expecting their fifth child. This child is **John Wesley**, founder of Methodism.

2. A young man is a victim of a number of serious health problems, and his wife has tuberculosis. Of their four children, one is blind, one has died, one is deaf, and one has tuberculosis. Now the woman finds that she is pregnant again, and the child is born deaf. That child is **Ludwig Von Beethoven,** composer of the Fifth and Ninth Symphonies.

3. As the result of a rape by a white man, a thirteen-year old black girl is pregnant. The unborn child is **Ethel Waters**, famous gospel singer who sings the song "His Eye Is on the Sparrow."

4. In a society where sexual propriety is regarded as essential, a teenage girl is pregnant, and her betrothed is not the father. This child is **Jesus Christ** (Reid, 2002, 56-57).

Due to the present-day era of postmodernism, each one of these cases could result in an abortion due to the calculation of inconvenience, health concerns, and lack of resources. Pro-choice advocates would say that the biblical stand on these scenarios is not relevant because people today have choices that were not available then. The use of alternatives would equate that there is no absolute right answer to these scenarios. However, what is not stated is that abortion goes against GOD's commandments. One of the Ten Commandments found in **Exodus 20:13** states, *Thou shalt not kill,* but we legislate abortion, which is uncontested murder. The infant, not an embryo, does not get a vote or choice whether to live or die. All humans start at this stage of development; therefore, from day 1 of fertilization through germination development, the cell is an infant. A chicken is a chicken whether it's in or out of the egg. Abortion goes against GOD's purpose because Scripture states in **Jeremiah 1:5** *Before I [GOD] formed thee in the belly I [GOD] knew thee; and before thou camest forth out of the womb I*

[GOD] sanctified thee, and I [GOD] ordained thee a prophet unto the nations. GOD has a purpose for the every one before while they are in their mother's womb.

Postmodern ideology has had impacts on American society. The family structure has changed, and the activities of parents play in their children's lives has changed. Research from the American Family Association shows:

- "Only 34 percent of America's families eat one meal together each day.
- The average father spends only eight to ten minutes a day with his children. This includes television and mealtimes.
- Only 12 percent of America's families pray together.
- The average couple spends only four minutes of uninterrupted time together a day" (Pipes & Lee, 1999, 6).

This postmodern view promotes pragmatisms with it's containerize perspective concerning your truth is not my truth. This anonymity of individualism is the root cause concerning relativity and no absolute truth that is corrupting the American Society, thereby causing the family structure to deteriorate. Pragmatism is the ideology that supports there are not absolute truth, meaning truth lies solely in practical result (Erickson, 1998, 43). The consequences of sin within postmodern ideas will definitely affect the future generations of America. This new idea of tolerance directly conflicts with the Christian-Believer beliefs that there is one GOD and one way of living. Postmodernism wants everyone to feel free to do whatever "feels" good, provides enjoyment, or is entertaining without consideration for anyone else.

The Christian-Believer who embraces the Bible will always seek the Bible for guidance and direction; however, modern society will tell the Christian-Believer that their belief system is only relevant to an individual person not to society. The "anonymity about ideology sphere facilitates the acceptance of new values by diminishing their significant. The pragmatism of represents wherever anonymity increases accountability decreases" (Wells, 1994, 10). This section again reiterates how we as Christian-Believers must be vigilant concerning Satan tricks and devices because people are **PLAYIN A GAME AND DON'T KNOW THE RULES: The Reality of Christianity.**

Matthew 9:6
But That Ye May Know That The Son Of Man Hath Power On Earth To Forgive Sins, (Then Saith HE To The Sick Of The Palsy,) Arise, Take Up Thy Bed, And Go Unto Thine House.

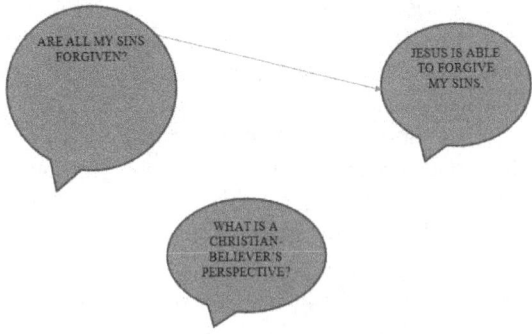

Redemption is for those who repent and turn from their sins. This Atonement is for all those who accept Jesus Christ as their Lord over their lives and Savior over sin. **John 15:6:** *Jesus saith unto him, I am the way, the truth, and the life; no man cometh to the Father but by ME.*

ATONEMENT

Jesus Christ is the propitiation of sins. Salvation is one distinction of Christianity that separates it from other religious faiths. Christian-Believers uphold the theology that GOD sent HIS only son from Heaven to the earth in human form to be the sacrifice for all. *Christ died for sinners* (**1 Timothy 1:15**; **Romans 5:6–8**). The sacrifice made by Jesus Christ is the Atonement. The Atonement of sin is why Christ died; salvation is a derivative. Salvation is the gift from GOD because of the Atonement. The following is a weakness of Calvinism and Arminian doctrine. The Calvinist's understanding of Christ describes Christ death as being for the elect. In Arminian theology, there is no Original Sin. This approach is theologically important to address the popular salvation theories. In the book, *Theology for Today,* Dr. Towns discusses the weakness in the definition of salvation from Calvinist and Arminian perspectives (Towns, 2001, 43):

Calvinist:
- Total Depravity
- Predestination
- Limited Atonement

Arminian:
- No Original Sin
- Limited Definition of Sin

- Completed Work of Christ

Explanation of Weaknesses in Theories of Atonement:

- **Total Depravity**: This tends to lead toward total inability among people to choose Jesus Christ as their Lord and Savior. This inability of humans goes against **2 Peter 3:10,** which says, *The Lord is not slack concerning, HIS promise, as some men count slackness; but is longsuffering to us-ward, not willing that any should perish, but that all should come to repentance.* Notice the Scripture says, *"not willing that any should perish,"* which means there are those who will perish for not repenting and receiving salvation through Jesus Christ. Repentance is an act you must do yourself; no one can repent for your sins except you. Jesus came that you may have life and have life more abundantly, but HE requires that you ask and seek (**Matthew 7:7**).

- **Predestination:** If everything were predetermined, then why would GOD tell the disciples, *And, being assembled together with them, commanded them that they should not depart from Jerusalem, but wait for the promise of the Father, which, saith HE, ye have heard of ME* (**Acts 1:4**)? If the "elect" are already chosen, then what is the need to evangelize? The Hebrews who left with Moses are the peculiar people not everyone that is of Hebrew descendant. The tribe of Judah and the tribes who stayed with Judah are called Jews (the name "Jew" is a slang from the word Judah given during the time of Babylonian captivity) and their descendants lived in Jerusalem and Judaea. The Samaritans were "half-breeds." In Scripture, everyone who is not a Jew/Hebrew is a Gentile.

When Jesus comes back, HE is going to the country of Israel in the city of Jerusalem, not anywhere in the United States, not anywhere in Europe, not anywhere in Africa, not anywhere in Asia, or any other nation state, city, or continent. If predetermination is accurate, it pushes everyone who is not from the line of Jacob (i.e. Israel), who left with Moses out of Egypt, who are in the Tribe of Judah or under the tribe of Judah after David out of salvation to Heaven. Remember, the thieves on the cross with Jesus were Jews not Gentiles. We know this because Jesus did not have a ministry with Gentiles but rather the lost children of Israel. Jesus ministry geography mainly composed of areas in Jerusalem, Galilee, and Judea areas. It was HIS disciples in **Acts 1:8** *But ye shall receive* ***power, after that the Holy Ghost*** (i.e. Holy Spirit) *is come upon you (NO POWER, NO MINISTRY WITHOUT THE HOLY SPIRIT): and you shall be*

> *MY witnesses both in Jerusalem, and in all Judea, and in Samaria, and unto the uttermost part of the earth.*

- **Denial of Original Sin:** This teaching goes against **Romans 3:23** *For all have sinned, and come short of the glory of GOD.* Remember it is in Genesis when GOD curses Adam. GOD told Adam, *Cursed is the ground for thy sake.* Adam was born from the ground (**Genesis 2:7**); therefore, his descendants are from the ground. This means that all descendants of Adam have sin from birth until death. Notice that Jesus Christ was not born of the seed of a man but from the Holy Spirit and the egg of a woman. If at any time, on any universe, at any dimension in space, any person can go a day without sinning, then Jesus Christ died in vain. If you can be "sinless" one day, then you can be sinless through eternity.

Atonement approaches the fundamental that is critical for Christian-Believers to understand. The three common views of Atonement are the ransom theory, the Anselmian theory, and the Abelardian theory. The ransom theory, first proposed by Origen (c.185–254 AD), was developed from **Mark 10:45** and explained the Atonement as a price paid by GOD in Christ to the devil. St. Anselm (c.1033–1109 AD) explained the Atonement as an act of satisfaction paid by Christ for man to GOD, who demanded from man perfect obedience to the law, which he could not fulfill because of his sinfulness. The theory of Peter Abelard (1079–1142 AD) viewed Christ's death as an inspiring appeal of love evoking in the sinner a response of love, thus removing his sin" (Hamburger, 1855).

Key Points

- Christ died not just to make salvation possible but also to actually show that GOD is more powerful even in death.
- To make an Atonement for one is to make satisfaction for his offenses (**Exodus 32:30; Leviticus 4:26; 5:16; Numbers 6:11**), and, as regarding the person, to reconcile, to propitiate to GOD on man's behalf.
- Christ's work consisted of suffering and obedience, and these were vicarious—i.e., were not merely for our benefit, but were in our stead, as the suffering and obedience of our vicar, or substitute.
- The Atonement is not the cause but the consequence of GOD's love to the guilty (**John 3:16; Romans 3:24, 25; Ephesians 1:7; 1 John 1:9; 4:9**).
- There are no conditions to be met in order to be saved outside of repentance and faith because Paul writes in **Ephesians 2:8-9** *For by*

grace are ye saved through faith; and
not of yourselves: it is the gift of GOD:
⁹ Not of works lest any man should
boast.

- Salvation is not a human
achievement. In the Old Testament,
sacrifice is a major contribution but
not because of any merit it has of
itself (**Hebrews 10:4**), but rather
because GOD has given it as the way
(**Lev. 17:11**).

Dr. Towns does a good job of explaining
respective areas of Calvinism and Arminianism;
however, in each case they leave the reader
with blanks concerning Atonement. Christian-
Believers of today are not concerned about
titles (i.e. 1- and 2-point Calvinist) but rather
the meanings behind their faith, the correlation
between the Old and New Testament, and
seeing GOD's purpose for humanity being
fulfilled. It is the Atonement that Christ died
for, not salvation. Salvation is by grace and not
of work lest any man should boast—it is a gift
from GOD. The Atonement shows the love of
GOD in action for humanity. Information is
important for comprehension; however, without
an ending statement or synopsis, the data can
be mute in the scope of analysis.

Finally, Dr. Towns does not expound
on obedience and sacrifice of Christ for the
Atonement. Jesus Christ was the sacrificial lamb;

however, it was HIS obedience to GOD that shows the significance and parallelism to the Old Testament. Samuel told Saul in **1 Samuel 15:22** *And Samuel said, Hath the LORD [as great] delight in burnt offerings and sacrifices, as in obeying the voice of the LORD? Behold, to obey [is] better than sacrifice…*Jesus Christ was also under this same law of obedience. **Luke 22:42** *Saying, Father, if thou be willing, remove this cup from me: nevertheless, not my will, but thine, be done.* These Scriptures illuminate how important obedience is to GOD. This section again reiterates how, without the Holy Spirit to guide us, we as Christian-Believers are **PLAYIN A GAME AND DON'T KNOW THE RULES: The Reality of Christianity.**

MARK 3:27

No Man Can Enter A Strong Man's House And Spoil His Goods Unless He First Binds The Strong Man.

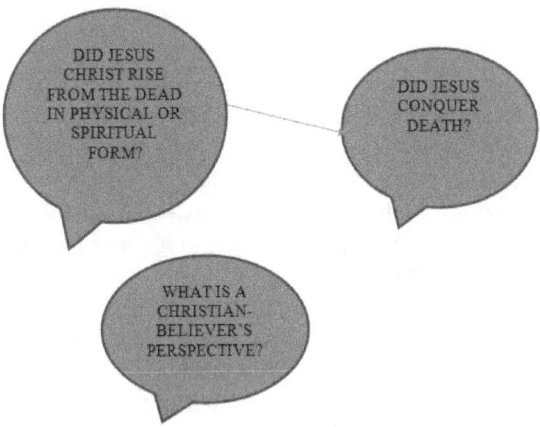

DID JESUS CHRIST RISE FROM THE DEAD IN PHYSICAL OR SPIRITUAL FORM?

DID JESUS CONQUER DEATH?

WHAT IS A CHRISTIAN-BELIEVER'S PERSPECTIVE?

We as Christian-Believers serve a GOD that has the power over all creation. In these last days, GOD has spoken unto us through HIS Son, whom HE hath appointed heir of all things living and non-living, by whom also HE made the worlds. Jesus Christ is the Son of GOD as part of the triune Deity.

BODILY RESURRECTION

There are those who state that Paul and the gospels in the New Testament are in contradiction concerning the resurrection of Jesus Christ. The motivation behind only physicalizing Christ runs deeper than a theological debate; it is a doctrinal foundation disruption for not establishing the spiritual and physical (i.e. tangible) of HIS resurrection. If Jesus Christ did not resurrect physically, then the gospels are in error. The New Testament would not be inspired revelation and a true representation of the historical actuality of Jesus Christ's ministry.

One argument concerns Jesus Christ's resurrection being physical or spiritual. This argument is circular since it states that Paul equates his "view" with the view of the disciples, and that if his view is non-physical, then the appearance of Jesus to the disciples was non-physical. The twelve original Disciples of Christ had a physical manifestation of Jesus Christ, and Paul had a supernatural experience. Paul and the disciples may have been different modes of transmission; however, both were from Christ. Since GOD is omnipotent and omnipresent, HE is not limited to any mode of transmission. GOD can appear in a vision (**Ezekiel 11:24**), a dream (**Genesis 31:24**), in person (i.e. Matthew, Mark, Luke, John), through an animal (**Numbers 22:28**), and audibly (**1 Samuel 3:10**). The ability of GOD to communicate as HE sees fit refutes the argument that Christ only has one manifestation form. Having a personal experience with Jesus Christ is the main objective. GOD is completely independent from man's scrutiny, and HE decides what form of communication to use.

Docetism denies the resurrection of Christ in a historical capacity. The validity of Docetism is not accurate because its "theological and philosophical reflection" came after the Jewish tradition written in the Hebrew Bible and therefore is subservient and not the authority. Docetism is "the assertion that Christ's human body was a phantasm, and that HIS suffering and death were mere appearance" (Hindson & Caner, 2008, 179).

Docetism does not accept Christ's incarnation; therefore; their understanding of Christianity and being a Christian-Believer is blurred and distorted. Their theological reflection of Christ is the basis of heresy because it does not agree with the early Church. The Church rejects heresy and therefore rejects the Docetism concept of Jesus's physical resurrection.

Bottom line, a Christian-Believer accepts all sixty-six books of the Bible. The Bible is not from the ideology of permission but rather on authority. A Christian-Believer's lifestyle must reflect all sixty-six books. The twenty-first century Church is **PLAYIN A GAME AND DON'T KNOW THE RULES: The Reality of Christianity.**

PART IV
CHRISTIAN-BELIEVER
COMPREHENSION

Job 13:15
Though HE Slay Me, Yet Will I Trust HIM And Maintain My Ways Before HIM

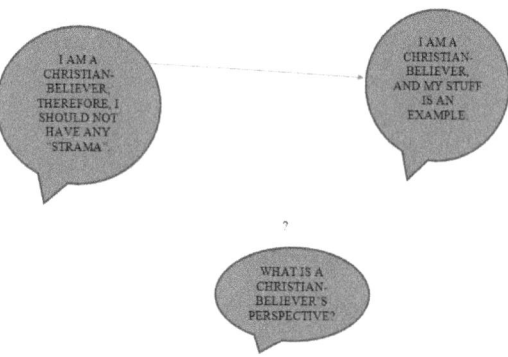

Being a Christian-Believer means putting Christ's requirements and commands before your own desires and self-will (i.e. yourself). Christian-Believers have only one entitlement, and that is GOD's love. Everything else is a blessing from GOD. Just as not all members are apostles, not all members will be financially independent and "strama" (stress + drama) free.

THE UNTOLD MESSAGE OF JOB

The book of Job is among the books of Wisdom in both the Christian and Hebrew Bibles. Wisdom comes at a cost, but lack of wisdom costs more. In the book of Job, GOD initiates a conversation with Satan concerning Job, and the first thing GOD mentions about Job involves the righteous character of Job (**Job 1–2**). This desired character, however, does not obviate chastisement, nor does it give Job any preferential treatment with GOD. Many Christlike persons quote the book of Job as a book about "double for my trouble, welcoming hardship because I am guaranteed abundant blessings from GOD." These Christlike persons state that Job's message is how GOD will bless HIS children in the end with the desires of their heart. This "candy" perception is very far from the true message of the book of Job. These persons miss the significance of this book and Job's theological message to the Church.

The book of Job is Wisdom for the Church. The primary teaching of Job's wisdom is not about remaining patient and GOD will bless you with substance at the end of your trials. This is the twenty-first century Christlike understanding. The real wisdom is that Job shows us how to maintain appropriate behavior and the right attitude during trying times.

As Christian-Believers, we are to live life blameless and with integrity. We are to welcome adversity from the enemy because we know that GOD is in charge. **Romans 5:3–5** *And not only so, but we glory in tribulations also: knowing that tribulation worketh patience; ⁴And patience, experience; and experience, hope: ⁵And hope maketh not ashamed; because the love of GOD is shed abroad in our hearts by the Holy Ghost, which is given unto us.* I am not saying that Christian-Believers do not make mistakes and fall into temptation, but these mistakes should not be glamorized at Church. We should strive to teach everyone away from these same mistakes; otherwise, we are giving negative reinforcement of deficient behavior that costs— and not just in a monetary value. Negative reinforcement is to give attention or highlight behavior that is contrary to the Holy WORD of GOD.

The wisdom of the book of Job is deeper than receiving blessings from GOD. This book reveals that the character of a person is the most important attribute. GOD commended Job as being of blameless character (**Job 1**). The second lesson in the book of Job shows GOD's reasoning when man questions His actions (i.e.

Job). The message from GOD to all humanity is regardless of your "blameless life and character"; the will of GOD has precedence.

The book of Job informs the Christian-Believer of GOD's response to those who question HIS authority on decisions for humanity. To question GOD is unacceptable and worthy of GOD's wrath. When we question what GOD is doing, we are putting ourselves as being equal to GOD just like Lucifer tried to do (**Isaiah 14:12–17**), which did not end well. Being narcissistic (i.e. exaggerated self-importance) and having an egocentric (i.e. selfishness) mentality leads to such shallow self-awareness when serving GOD (i.e. causality). This misunderstanding of the GODhead represents that Job has layers of ridiculousness deep-fried in confusion. GOD created the universe without any guidance or assistance from any human; therefore, GOD is not required to answer or request permission from anyone to do anything of his good pleasure.

Job 38 is GOD's response to the internal and external questioning of Job. This questioning by Job is indirectly degrading GOD and HIS actions to the human scrutiny. This questioning behavior exhibited by Job is unacceptable to GOD. The LORD quickly stops this foolishness by presenting scenarios in which Job has neither the knowledge nor understanding. The first question GOD asks Job is *who is this that darkeneth counsel by words without knowledge* (**Job 38:2**). This question is a direct reflection of how GOD views the audacity of Job with his human pride to question what GOD is doing. The Lord may be refuting Job's apparent contention that GOD's relationship to man was a juridical relationship in which GOD was obligated to repay him. The refutation of this dogma aids in the demolition of its corollary (which undergirds ancient Near Eastern religions) that man's relationship to GOD is based on a juridical claim (Parsons, 1981).

Gird up now thy loins like a man; for I will demand of thee, and answer thou (**Job 38:3**) is a caution statement from GOD giving Job a warning to prepare for battle. When men needed freedom to work, run, or fight, they would tuck the hem of the tunic into the girdle to gain greater freedom and movement. This action was called "girding up the loins," and the phrase became a metaphor for preparedness (Price, 2007).

The next is a statement from GOD for straight hand-to-hand combat, (**Job 38:4**). *Where wast thou when I laid the foundations of the earth? Declare, if thou hast understanding.*" Job is probably unaware of the water cycle process let alone physics of the earth. The questions that follow from GOD to Job reveals inadequacy in Job's thinking that he had the juridical claim with GOD's decisions. GOD shows the ineptness of Job's knowledge and understandings.

When HE asks the question, GOD's omniscience far exceeds the intellect of man. "Satan, Eliphaz, Bildad, Zophar, and to some extent Job wrongly assumed that punishment of the wicked and reward of the righteous in this life is a fixed doctrine" (Waters, 1997). Once GOD illuminates to Job his position in relation to GOD, Job begins to regret and repent for his illiteracy (**Job 42:6**). Job's repentance is not a confession of sin but rather the acknowledgement and acceptance of a newly discovered vocation, to follow and emulate the GOD of the Hebrews (Shelley, 1992).

The book of Job represents the true righteousness of GOD. The word righteous is a "Hebrew word *saddiq,* which means straight or right" (Elwell 2001, 1033). The definition illustrates that the actions of GOD are without error or compromise. This is the lesson that Job learned. Job's initial understanding of GOD's grace and blessings are linear (i.e. mathematical) motivated by GOD's enjoyment of Job's righteousness and constant reverence to HIM. The "righteousness" that Job understood caused him and others to think that there are entitlements from GOD and exemptions to life trials.

Job misunderstood that GOD motivates GOD and Job's obedience gave him favor, not immunity. Righteousness is subjective to how GOD interprets it. GOD is righteousness; therefore, in order to understand righteousness, you must first understand GOD. Job's righteousness was according to man's standards of his day, but GOD is the validator of such a title.

Job performed sacrifices to ensure GOD's blessing. **Job 1:6** ... *It may be that my sons have sinned, and cursed GOD in their hearts. Thus, Job did continually.* Job learns through his trials that human righteousness does not equate to GOD's blessings; rather, GOD's love for HIS children motivates HIM to give blessings. GOD's permeation of love is not always in ways that are conducive to our human understanding or lifestyle.

Job declares in **Job 3:25** *For the thing that which I greatly feared is come upon me*, which shows that Job did not actually trust GOD with his substance. Fear was the motivation behind Job's sacrifices to GOD rather than the love and worship toward the GOD of all the earth. It is this emotion of fear that GOD saw in Job and Satan's discontentment against humanity that GOD used to cleanse Job of his fear. At all times GOD was in control of the situation. God initiates a conversation with Satan concerning Job, and the first thing God mentions about Job in both places involves Job's character (Thompson, 2006, 1). However, GOD wanted Satan to think that he, Satan, had moved GOD against HIS wishes, but GOD will not be moved until HE wants to be moved.

When GOD speaks of Job, it reminds Satan, the once archangel, that there are those of GOD's creations who live according to GOD's WORDs. GOD echoes Job's reputation in the whole earth concerning his upright character. GOD **allowed** Satan to bring tragedies to Job's life because GOD knew that these things would bring Job to the true understanding of GOD and HIS righteousness. This illustrates that Satan has no power on his own. Satan needs permission to tempt Job on three critical points of his life: family, finances, and health. Satan understood that humans value these things. It is in these areas that Satan thought he could bring Job to his breaking point and curse GOD. These attacks on family, finances, and health reveal to Christian-Believers an understanding of the areas where Satan can influence your life with people decisions that affect your life; however, Satan cannot take your soul or life and as long as the person is living, there is hope. **Ecclesiastes 9:4** *For to his that is joined to all the living there is hope: for a living dog is better than a dead lion.*

In the final chapters of the book, Job begins to understand himself and his superficial reality of his relationship with GOD. The Scripture that gave this manifestation of Job's superficial relationship is **Job 3:25** *For thing I greatly feared the most is come upon me, and that which I was afraid of is come unto me.* Job learned through his circumstances that the righteousness base is GOD and that "whatever GOD does is just and right simply because HE does it" (Erickson, 1998, 443). It is man's destiny to emulate GOD's righteousness and not GOD to esteem righteousness to be like man. "GOD wants to prevent Job from clutching his claim… [where] he [Job] places his innocence above GOD's purity" (LaSor, Hubbard & Bush, 1996, 482). Job now understood that burnt offerings are part of the destiny of purification towards GOD righteousness, and the laws that GOD imposes on humanity literally do not apply to HIM (Erickson, 1998, 443). Our job is to trust the sovereignty of GOD because HE is GOD.

In conclusion, the book of Job at the superficial level promotes that patience through circumstances can bring monetary awards from GOD; however, with further research one finds that there is a deeper and more spiritually enriched meaning. The book of Job shows the traditional Eastern Religion interpretation, in which "GOD" is obligated to perform certain acts for HIS people based upon their obedience; Job was able to see the trueness of GOD's character. The righteousness that Job thought he had was based upon his understanding that if I continue to do "works," then GOD will bless me. GOD wanted to demonstrate to Job that it was not Job's "works" that motivated GOD to provide success in Job's life but rather it was GOD's love and sovereign rule over the earth.

Job initially served GOD with the understanding that GOD, the creator of Heaven and Earth, had limitation on HIS ability to allocate resources; therefore, he had to continue those offerings in order to keep blessings for his family. Job thought his righteousness was the reason for the blessing. When Job went through his trials, he never cursed GOD; however, he began to question why things happened to him. Job did not understand that as he questioned GOD's existence, he also questioned GOD's supremacy. Once GOD revealed to Job the true nature of who GOD is in comparison to man, Job began to see that all that a man has is GOD. The family, finances, and health are streams by which GOD blessed him because HE is the GOD of all universes. GOD is the ruler over all things living and non-living.

GOD speaks atoms, GOD speaks all human languages, GOD speaks molecules, GOD speaks locust, GOD speaks frogs, GOD speaks water, GOD speaks moon, GOD speaks sun, GOD speaks clouds, GOD speaks whale, GOD speaks fish, alligator, GOD speaks wood, GOD speaks paper, GOD speaks tree, and any other thing in existence. Job's repentance was not from a conscious sin of commission or omission but rather an unconscious sin of ignorance. Job's previous understanding of obedience and refuting sin was through fear with misunderstanding of the vast power of the GOD he serves. After Job's trial, he understood that serving GOD with obedience is because HE loves us and will protect us from all because HE is GOD for real. Being a Christian-Believer means putting Christ's requirements and commands before your own desires and self-will (i.e. yourself). Christian-Believers have only one entitlement, and that is GOD's love. Everything else is a blessing, grace, and mercy from GOD. Just as not all members are apostles, not all members will be financially independent and "strama"-free. The book of Job again reveals we are **PLAYIN A GAME AND DON'T KNOW THE RULES: The Reality of Christianity.**

ACTS 1:8

But Ye Shall Receive Power, After That The Holy Ghost Is Come Upon You: And Ye Shall Be Witnesses Unto Me Both In Jerusalem, And In All Judaea, And In Samaria, And Unto The Uttermost Part Of The Earth.

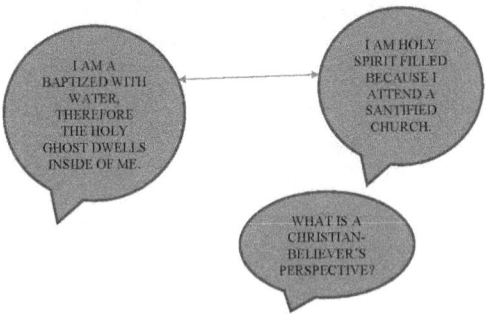

Being a Christian-Believer means putting Christ's requirements and commands—such as fear GOD and keep HIS commandment, for it is the whole duty of man (**Ecclesiastes 12:13**), and love one another as I have loved you (**John 13:34**)—before all things, including the desires and will of the self. Christian-Believers must

tarry for the Holy Ghost. **Luke 24:49** *And,
behold, I send the promise of my Father upon you:
but tarry ye in the city of Jerusalem, until ye be
endued with power from on high.*

THE HOLY SPIRIT

Ephesians 4:11–12 *And he gave some,*
apostles; and some, prophets; and
some, evangelists; and some, pastors
and teachers; ¹² For the perfecting of the
Saints, for the work of the ministry, for the
edifying of the body of Christ

Evidence of the indwelling of Holy Spirit is
with speaking in tongues, there is no other way.
The Holy Spirit can use anyone or anything at
any time for a purpose (i.e. donkey with Balaam,
Elisabeth, etc.), but HIS indwelling presence is
another level that requires sacrifice, obedience,
and commitment through tarrying in prayer like
the disciples did in Jerusalem. The disciples spent
days or possibly weeks in prayer before the Day
of Pentecost according to **Acts 1:4-5** *And, being*
assembled together with them, commanded them
that they should not depart from Jerusalem, but
wait for the promise of the Father, which, saith HE,
ye have heard of ME. ⁵ For John truly baptized with
water; but ye shall be baptized with the Holy Ghost
not many days hence. The Holy Spirit baptism is a
separate baptism from water baptism.

Jesus went through the water baptism
by John the Baptist to fulfill all righteousness
(**Matthew 3:15**) because HE was without sin.
Jesus Christ disciples went through water
baptism but they did not receive the indwelling

of the Holy Spirit. Notice how Jesus Christ went down in the water and when HE came up out of the water the Holy Spirit descended upon HIM like a dove. These are two separate events for two separate purposes. Water Baptism is repentance for the remittance of sin (**Mark 1:4**) and Holy Ghost baptism is for power (**Acts 1:8**) over the enemy through the Gifts, Callings, and Fruit of the Holy Spirit. Jesus disciples' baptized people while they were with HIM, which was water baptism of John the Baptist for repentance but HE did not (**John 4:2**). Paul also identifies Water Baptism is for repentance, **Acts 19:4** *Then said Paul, John verily baptized with the baptism of repentance, saying unto the people, that they should believe on him which should come after HIM, that is, on Christ Jesus.*

The following Scriptures support the separation of baptisms. It is at the Day of Pentecost that the disciples of Jesus Christ received the indwelling of the Holy Spirit with evidence of Speaking in Tongues, **Acts 2:4** *And they were all filled with the Holy Ghost, and began to speak with other tongues, as the Spirit gave them utterance.* Peter while giving the WORD of GOD to Cornelius, the Holy Spirit came with evidence of Speaking in Tongues, **Acts 10:46** *For they heard them speak with tongues, and magnify* GOD. Paul, while visiting the Ephesians, lays hands on them and they begin to Speak in Tongues, **Acts 19:6** *And when Paul had laid his hands upon them* [Ephesians], *the Holy Ghost came on them; and they spake with tongues, and prophesied.* Speaking in tongues through the indwelling of GOD the Holy Spirit has nothing to do with salvation, but rather it is evidence of the indwelling of the Holy Spirit with HIS power. Jesus went through this process of Water Baptism and the indwelling of the Holy Spirit to show Christian-Believers the process needed for 1) Salvation and 2) Holy Spirit power through the Gifts, Callings, and Fruit.

The Holy Spirit is the third being of the Trinity. The Holy Spirit did not appear unto man until the Day of Pentecost. "Up to that time the Spirit had not been given, since Jesus had not yet been glorified" (Morrison, 2007). GOD the Holy Spirit's mission is to declare to the world the active portion of the GODhead through manifestation of callings, gifts, and fruit within their creation. Irenaeus of Lyons is highly respected because was a disciple of Polycarp. It is Irenaeus that said, Humankind is to be instructed not only by ANGELS, but also by two hands of GOD: the WORD and the Holy Spirit (Gonzalez, 1984, 68-69). This quote by Irenaeus shows the high regard he and his predecessors gave to the Holy Spirit. Polycarp was a disciple known for his speech in persecution. During the period of the persecution of the Church, a judge stated to the bailiff to remove the atheist, referring to Polycarp, but Polycarp repeated those words to the crowd and said, "Out with these atheists!" (Gonzalez, 1984, 44) referring to the judge and his council.

The Holy Spirit, whom GOD the Father will send in Jesus Christ's name, is, according to **John 14:26,** the comforter (KJV), counselor (Christian Standard Bible [CSB]), advocate (NIV), friend (MSG), and helper (ESV). This grace given by GOD would manifest through the gifts of the Holy Spirit. Thus, charisma is for the purpose of service or the furthering of ministry and is described as a manifestation of divine power (Dominy, 2010). There are three common Greek terms used to describe the Spirit's gifts. They are charismata, diakoniai, and energermata. "Charismata designate 'that which is bestowed by GOD's favor, freely, and graciously given.' Diakoniai means services or ministries. Energermata means workings or energies. The filling of the Holy Spirit appears to be a state in which the Holy Spirit for service controls a person (Lea & Black, 2003, 292) by permission.

The Holy Spirit's gifts have purposes. The word "gift," used by the Apostle Paul, refers to a variety of aspects of the Holy Spirit. The Spirit manifestation is to strengthen, edify, teach, or put into action. This understanding shows that not all gifts of the Spirit are visible with outward signs. Scripture does mention that the Spiritual gifts are a sign of love from GOD. This equates to Christian-Believers being able to have the Holy Spirit. Its manifestations may not visible for all to see, but GOD knows. Remember **Romans 11:29** *The Gifts and Callings of GOD are without repentance.* GOD chooses our Gifts and Calling, we are responsible to adhere to and accept them according to GOD's purpose.

The Calling from the Holy Spirit

Ephesians 4:11-12 *And he gave some, apostles; and some; prophets; and some, evangelists; and some, pastors and teachers.* [12] *For the perfecting of the Saints, for the work of the ministry, for edifying of the body of Christ.*

The offices of the Church that Paul identifies with Ephesians are the leadership positions in the twenty-first century Church. The Spirit endowed the early kings of Israel with special capabilities (Erickson, 1998, 884). Many have forgotten the example of the apostles who sought guidance on positions. Unless GOD grants an individual the power to declare what HE is doing in the world, the person is not walking in control (Wells, 1994, 182).

The apostles were men with lives apart from ministry that Jesus Christ chose to establish HIS Church. **John 15:16** *Ye have not chosen me, but I have chosen you, and ordained you, that ye should go and bring forth fruit, and that your fruit should remain: that whatsoever ye shall ask of the Father in my name, HE may give it unto you.*

Paul mentions these spiritual gifts in order of precedence. The first being the apostle, by which Jesus chose the first twelve. There are diverse gifts of apostles, prophets, and others in the Church. Paul wants us to catch the vision of one Church (Carson & Moo 2005, 496). This vision is the heartbeat of GOD concerning HIS work on the earth. The question then arises whether the office of apostleship is limited to the first-century Church. If the Holy Spirit is the same yesterday, today, and forevermore, why would the manifestation of the Holy Spirit would be different between Biblical times and today.

Jesus Christ selected the twelve disciples in **Mark 3:13–19**

> *And HE goeth up into a mountain, and calleth unto HIM whom HE would: and they came unto HIM. [14] And HE ordained twelve, that they should be with HIM, and that HE might send them forth to preach, [15] And to have power to heal sicknesses, and to cast*

out devils: ¹⁶ And Simon HE surnamed
Peter; ¹⁷ And James the son of Zebedee,
and John the brother of James; and HE
surnamed them Boanerges, which is,
the sons of thunder: ¹⁸ And Andrew,
and Philip, and Bartholomew, and
Matthew, and Thomas, and James the
son of Alphaeus, and Thaddeus, and
Simon the Canaanite, ¹⁹And Judas
Iscariot, which betrayed HIM: and they
went into an house.

Did you not notice that there are three sets
of brothers within the apostle ranks? Simon and
Andrew are brothers, Peter being the oldest.
James and John, with James being the older
of the two, also called James the Elder, are the
sons of Zebedee. Matthew (tax collector, the Levi
[**Mark 2:14**]) and James, called James the Less,
are sons of Alphaeus. The author of the book of
James in the Bible is James, the brother of Jesus,
who is called James the Just. James the Just
is the **FIRST BISHOP ordained in Jerusalem**
(Acts 15:2 and read The Works of Eusebius).
James was appointed by the Apostles (Eusebius
records this action).

In addition, if the person by name is
not referenced as an apostle in the Bible,
then he/she is not an apostle. The Bible does
not conform to this or any other century's

standards. There were fourteen apostles in the New Testament (the original twelve, Matthias, and Paul)—no more and no less. There are apostles and prophets in the twenty-first century because if there are no more apostles and prophets, then there are no longer any evangelists, pastors, or teachers. It is not a three-fold ministry but five-fold. GOD does not change, **Hebrews 13:8** *Jesus Christ the same yesterday, and today, and forever.* Since Jesus Christ, GOD the Son, is the same, and HE and GOD the Father are one, and GOD the Holy Spirit with GOD the Father and GOD the Son make the GODhead. The Trinity exists from **Genesis 1:1** until present, so the Callings, Gifts, and Fruit of GOD the Spirit exist today.

The Apostle

Apostles are different from prophets, evangelists, pastors, and teachers. Apostles have GOD's authority for establishing Churches and are the channels of divine revelation. They are the ones to establish Churches and place pastors in Churches over GOD's sheep. Apostles are like the thumb on a hand. Just as the thumb can touch all four other fingers, so too can the apostle operate in the prophetic, evangelical, pastoral, and teaching gifts. The apostle's main vision is through prayer and the ministry of establishing Churches. **Acts 6:2, 4** *Then the twelve called the multitude of the disciples unto them, and said, It is not reason that we should leave the WORD of GOD, and serve tables. ⁴ But we will give ourselves continually to prayer, and to the ministry of the WORD.* Apostle Christian-Believers in the twenty-first century are still establishing Churches and placing people.

It is the job of the apostle to put a person into position to watch over the sheep as shepherds (i.e. pastors), elders (i.e. teachers), and missionaries (i.e. evangelists). "The only people who can survive in pastoral ministry are those with the unmistakable call of GOD in their life" (Rainer, 2001, 55). Notice that apostles are matured Christian-Believers with actions that are transparent to the ways of the Bible, and their mission in ministry is building the Household of Faith for Jesus Christ. They are educated in Church theology, not necessarily formal education. Afterward, GOD selects apostles at their state of maturity in the faith of serving the GODhead. **Galatians 4:4** *But when the fullness of the time was come,* GOD *sent forth HIS Son, made of a woman, made under the law.* Apostles are not born but rather made through faithfulness and obedience to GOD's WORD.

The following are characteristics of some of the apostles in the Bible. **Peter** confers his faithfulness to not eating unclean things. **Acts**

10:14 *But Peter said, Not so, Lord; for I have never eaten anything that is common or unclean.* This declaration by Peter to Jesus Christ shows his commitment to the Law, which was meant to keep the children of Israel holy. **Leviticus 11:47** *To make a difference between the unclean and the clean, and between the beast that may be eaten and the beast that may not be eaten.* **Andrew**, Peter's younger brother, was a disciple of John the Baptist. **John 1:40** *One of the two which heard John speak, and followed HIM, was Andrew, Simon Peter's brother.*

John the Apsotle, the brother of James the Elder, was a disciple of John the Baptist also because he recounts of John the Baptist telling his disciples about Jesus. John could not have known this level of detail as firsthand experience. **John 1:36-37** *And looking upon Jesus as he walked, he saith, Behold the LAMB of GOD!* ³⁷ *And the two disciples heard HIM speak, and they followed Jesus.* **James** was called Boanerges with his brother John. **Mark 3:17** *And James the son of Zebedee, and John the brother of James; and he surnamed them Boanerges, which is, the sons of thunder.*

Peter, James, and John are special apostles to Jesus Christ. They are the first apostles mentioned. **Matthew 10:2:** *Now the names of the twelve apostles are these; The first, Simon, who* *is called Peter, and Andrew his brother; James the son of Zebedee, and John his brother.* Jesus Christ set them apart from other disciples. **Matthew 17:1** *And after six days Jesus taketh Peter, James, and John his brother, and bringeth them up into an high mountain apart.* The Lord also gave them special names. **Mark 3:16–17** *And Simon HE surnamed Peter; [17] And James the son of Zebedee, and John the brother of James; and HE surnamed them Boanerges, which is, the sons of thunder.* These three individuals were always present with Jesus.

Paul, the fourteenth apostle, was a Roman citizen, formally educated in the Law of Moses by the esteemed elder Gamliel. Both his parents were of Hebrew descent, and he was ordained as a Pharisee. **Acts 22:3:** *I am verily a man, which am a Jew, born in Tarsus, a city in Cilicia, yet brought up in this city at the feet of Gamaliel, and taught according to the perfect manner of the law of the fathers, and was zealous toward GOD, as ye all are this day.* **Philippians 3: 4–6** *Though I might also have confidence in the flesh. If any other man thinketh that he hath whereof he might trust in the flesh, I more: [5] Circumcised the eighth day, of the stock of Israel, of the tribe of Benjamin, an Hebrew of the Hebrews; as touching the law, a Pharisee; [6] Concerning zeal, persecuting the Church; touching the righteousness which is in the law, blameless.*

The Prophet

The gift of prophecy is not the same as the office of the prophet. The gift of prophecy is the receiving of revelation knowledge, and this only happens sporadically according to the proportion of the Christian-Believer's faith. Prophecy is not frequent in the Christian-Believer, while it is continual in the office of the prophet. He and/ or she are is the eyes of GOD for past, present, and future events and receives wisdom and revelation knowledge as a normal occurrence from the GODhead. We see examples of the prophet in the Old and New Testaments. To be a prophet, an individual must have had a message from GOD in the form of special revelation with guidance regarding its declaration so that it would be accurate with the authority of GOD. The Bible teaches us the LORD will not do anything unless HE first reveals it unto HIS servant the prophet (**Amos 3:7**).

Prophets principally minister to the Church and are not limited to a specific geographic location or ethnicity. The prophet is not gender specific; there are both male and female prophets in the Old and New Testament. You cannot go to school to be a prophet; only GOD can call and empower the prophet. GOD the Spirit gives as it wills. To every prophet, the Spirit gives the word of wisdom and word of knowledge at minimum as evidence of the office and not the gift only.

Prophets are born prophets with ordination by GOD during conception or in person. GOD speaks to the prophet in supernatural ways concerning HIS purpose for them. **Exodus 3:3–5** *And Moses said, I will now turn aside, and see this great sight, why the bush is not burnt. ⁴ And when the Lord saw that he turned aside to see,* GOD *called unto him out of the midst of the bush, and said, Moses, Moses. And he said, Here am I. ⁵ And HE said, Draw not nigh hither: put off thy shoes from off thy feet, for the place whereon thou standest is holy ground.* GOD uses Moses in **Exodus 7** to show Pharaoh, the Egyptians, and the Hebrews that HE is ruler over all creation through the ten plagues of Egypt. In the book of Exodus, GOD reveals HE is supernatural by showing that HE not only speaks human languages but also insect (i.e. locust, flies), reptile, and amphibian (i.e. frogs) languages. GOD controls the atmospheric elements (i.e. turning water into blood) and can make living out of nonliving objects (i.e. rod turns into a snake and back to a rod). In **Exodus 7,** we also discover that GOD is the controller of the sun and moon (i.e. light and darkness).

The prophet Isaiah also had a supernatural experience with the GODhead seeking a representative on earth. **Isaiah 6:8** *Also I heard the voice of the Lord, saying, Whom shall I send, and who will go for US? Then said I, Here am I; send me.* Under HIS prophetic role, GOD gives Isaiah revelation of past, present, and current events. The past event concerns the motivation behind Lucifer's ejection from Heaven. **Isaiah 14:12–15** *How art thou fallen from Heaven, O Lucifer, son of the morning! how art thou cut down to the ground, which didst weaken the nations! ¹³ For thou hast said in thine heart, I will ascend into Heaven, I will exalt my throne above the stars of* GOD: *I will sit also upon the mount of the congregation, in the sides of the north: ¹⁴ I will ascend above the heights of the clouds; I will be like the most High. ¹⁵ Yet thou shalt be brought down to Hell, to the sides of the pit.*

The present events GOD reveals to Isaiah concern Hezekiah, Isaiah's fourth cousin. **Isaiah 38:1** *In those days was Hezekiah sick unto death. And Isaiah the prophet the son of Amoz came unto him, and said unto him, Thus saith the Lord, Set thine house in order: for thou shalt die, and not live.* Hezekiah repents, and GOD accepts Hezekiah's repentance and sends Isaiah back to him. **Isaiah 38:5** *Go, and say to Hezekiah, Thus saith the Lord, the GOD of David thy father, I have heard thy prayer, I have seen thy tears: behold, I will add unto thy days fifteen years.*

GOD reveals to Isaiah the deliverer of the Children of Israel is a Persian named Cyrus, one hundred and fifty years before he became a ruler. **Isaiah 44:28** *That saith of Cyrus, He is MY shepherd, and shall perform all MY pleasure: even saying to Jerusalem, Thou shalt be built; and to the temple, Thy foundation shall be laid.* It is to Isaiah that GOD reveals John the Baptist. **Isaiah 40:3** *The voice of him that crieth in the wilderness, Prepare ye the way of the LORD, make straight in the desert a highway for our* GOD [also mentioned in **Mark 1:2-3**]. HE also reveals to Isaiah the birth of Jesus Christ. **Isaiah 7:14** *Therefore the Lord himself shall give you a sign; Behold, a virgin shall conceive, and bear a son, and shall call HIS name Emmanuel / Immanuel.*

Jeremiah, the prophet, disrupts traditions of many nations, including Israel. Upon his ordination, GOD speaks to him in fact concerning their acquaintance. **Jeremiah 1:5** *Before I formed thee in the belly I knew thee; and before thou camest forth out of the womb I sanctified thee, and I ordained thee a prophet unto the nations.* Jeremiah is part of the tribes of Israel who sided with Judah when the separation of tribes occurred. **Jeremiah 1:1** *The words of Jeremiah the son of Hilkiah, of the priests that were in Anathoth in the land of Benjamin.* GOD comforts Jeremiah to not be afraid to speak the WORD of GOD. **Jeremiah 1:8-10**

Be not afraid of their faces: for I am with thee to deliver thee, saith the LORD.⁹ Then the LORD put forth HIS hand, and touched my mouth. And the LORD said unto me, Behold, I have put my words in thy mouth. ¹⁰ See, I have this day set thee over the nations and over the kingdoms, to root out, and to pull down, and to destroy, and to throw down, to build, and to plant.

Jeremiah rebukes the Hebrews for their backsliding ways. **Jeremiah 3:6-8**

The LORD said also unto me in the days of Josiah the king, Hast thou seen that which backsliding Israel hath done? she is gone up upon every high mountain and under every green tree, and there hath played the harlot. ⁷ And I said after she had done all these things, Turn thou unto me. But she returned not. And her treacherous sister Judah saw it. ⁸ And I saw, when for all the causes whereby backsliding Israel committed adultery I had put her away, and given her a bill of divorce; yet her treacherous sister Judah feared not, but went and played the harlot also.

GOD requires Jeremiah to remind HIS people of their treachery like an unfaithful wife. Jeremiah warns of people coming from afar whose language is not known to Israel (i.e. Babylonians). **Jeremiah 5:15** *Lo, I will bring a nation upon you from far, O house of Israel, saith the LORD: it is a mighty nation, it is an ancient nation, a nation whose language thou knowest not, neither understandest what they say.* Jeremiah warns against the tree used at Christmas. **Jeremiah 10:2–4** *Thus saith the Lord, Learn not the way of the heathen, and be not dismayed at the signs of Heaven; for the heathen are dismayed at them.* ³ *For the customs of the people are vain: for one cutteth a tree out of the forest, the work of the hands of the workman, with the axe.* ⁴ *They deck it with silver and with gold; they fasten it with nails and with hammers that it move not.* Yes, the Christmas tree has pagan not Christian-Believer origin.

Jeremiah also warns against the captivity by the Babylonians. **Jeremiah 25:9–11**

> *Behold, I will send and take all the families of the north, saith the LORD, and Nebuchadnezzar the king of Babylon, my servant, and will bring them against this land, and against the inhabitants thereof, and against all these nations round about, and will*

utterly destroy them, and make them an astonishment, and an hissing, and perpetual desolations. [10] Moreover I will take from them the voice of mirth, and the voice of gladness, the voice of the bridegroom, and the voice of the bride, the sound of the millstones, and the light of the candle. [11] And this whole land shall be a desolation, and an astonishment; and these nations shall serve the king of Babylon seventy years.

Jeremiah also speaks of the new covenant that will come through Jesus Christ. **Jeremiah 31: 31–33**

Behold, the days come, saith the Lord, that I will make a new covenant with the house of Israel, and with the house of Judah: [32] Not according to the covenant that I made with their fathers in the day that I took them by the hand to bring them out of the land of Egypt; which my covenant they brake, although I was an husband unto them, saith the Lord: [33] But this shall be the covenant that I will make with the house of Israel; After those days, saith the Lord, I will put my law in

> *their inward parts, and write it in their*
> *hearts; and will be their GOD, and they*
> *shall be my people.*

The life of John the Baptist and his supernatural acts of GOD begin early, **Luke 1:11–13**

> *And there appeared unto him an*
> *ANGEL of the LORD standing on the*
> *right side of the altar of incense. ¹²*
> *And when Zacharias saw him, he was*
> *troubled, and fear fell upon him. ¹³ But*
> *the ANGEL said unto him, Fear not,*
> *Zacharias: for thy prayer is heard; and*
> *thy wife Elisabeth shall bear thee a*
> *son, and thou shalt call his name John.*

This revelation concerning HIS name shows GOD has a purpose for John in the womb. The ANGEL of the LORD also declares John will be great in the sight of the GOD. **Luke 1:15** *For he shall be great in the sight of the Lord, and shall drink neither wine nor strong drink; and he shall be filled with the Holy Ghost, even from his mother's womb.* John the Baptist knew in the womb who the Messiah was while Mary was pregnant. **Luke 1:41–42** *And it came to pass, that, when Elisabeth heard the salutation of Mary, the babe leaped in her womb; and Elisabeth was filled with the Holy Ghost: ⁴² And* *she spake out with a loud voice, and said, Blessed art thou among women, and blessed is the fruit of thy womb.* John the Baptist was ordained at his ceremony of circumcision. **Luke 1:76** *And thou, child, shalt be called the prophet of the Highest: for thou shalt go before the face of the Lord to prepare HIS way.* John the Baptist's story reiterates that the call on the prophet begins at conception.

The Teacher

The calling to be a Teacher in the Church is not a calling by GOD given to every person. Within the Teacher callings, the Spirit GOD grants leadership in the Church. The Teacher is part of the five-fold ministry, and the gift of teaching comes from their calling. A person should not deduce that a schoolteacher is also called by Holy Spirit to hold the office of a Teacher in the Church. The schoolteacher makes a personal decision or choice to attend the university, receive a degree in education, and become a licensed teacher by a state board. The Teacher mentioned in the Bible is the office of a teacher; a person does not choose—GOD makes the decision.

The Teacher who is called by GOD teaches the WORD of GOD to the people of GOD. The Teacher of the Church does not score success as an academic achievement of A, B, C, D, etc. but rather through the people being taught ability to recite and implement the Bible's Scriptures with a mindset adjustment toward obedience and faith in the GODhead. Christian-Believers benefit from the Teacher's teaching the content and context of the Bible. The comprehension of the content and context of Scripture becomes evident in their daily lives with conversation and lifestyle choices.

The Teacher's role in the Church traces its roots to the days of the Old Testament scribes. We see Ezra as being called by GOD as a scribe (**Ezra 7:6**). Ezra took his calling to establish an educational system and teach the children of Israel the Mosaic Law after the children of Israel returned from exile. Being appointed a scribe and teaching GOD's WORD were not Ezra's own ideas of what he should be doing. Rather, Ezra was fulfilling the calling from GOD.

In the New Testament, Paul speaks of the Teacher in the same voice as with the apostle, prophet, evangelist, and pastor. Since Scripture teaches that the apostle, prophet, evangelist, and pastor are leadership positions in the Church, the Teacher by identification is also a leadership role within the Church. The Teacher's job is to teach the WORD of GOD. The Teacher's role is not to be the entertainer but to teach the undiluted, unedited WORD of GOD, which is sharper than any two-edged sword. In **Acts 20:7–12**, Luke writes about how when Paul was speaking, a man went to sleep and fell out of the window. Paul went to the brother and said life was still in him, went back into the upper-room, and continued his teaching. The role of the Teacher is to stand in an authoritative position in the Church to ensure the teaching is in accordance with Scripture and that members are rightly dividing the WORD of truth. Just because a person has a certification by a state board of education does not mean that the same person is a teacher as part of the five-fold ministry. The credentials of the Office of Teacher is upon their changing lives through education of the Scriptures. Man's standards are of the flesh; however, GOD's standards are spiritual. The Church is deceived and **PLAYIN A GAME AND DON'T KNOW THE RULES: The Reality of Christianity.** The Church does not understand that nothing that a person does apart from GOD is operating under the Holy Spirit but rather under man. A talent is not a gift of the Holy Spirit, nor is the manifestation of the nine gifts of the Holy Spirit a talent.

The Gifts from the Holy Spirit

1 Corinthians 12:8–10 *For to one is given by the Spirit of the word of wisdom; to*

> *another the word of knowledge by the same*
> *Spirit; 9) To another faith by the same*
> *Spirit; to another the gifts of healing by the*
> *same Spirit; 10) To another the working of*
> *miracles; to another prophecy; to another*
> *discerning of spirits; to another divers*
> *kinds of tongues; to another interpretation*
> *of tongues.*

"It is the work of the Holy Spirit to reveal the wisdom in the mystery of the cross" (Duggan, 1985). It is the book of **1 Corinthians** where many Christian-Believers focus a lot of attention, especially in the area of tongues. "Paul insists that it is not the phenomenon of "tongues" or prophesying in itself that gives evidence of the presence and activity of the Holy Spirit, but rather the actual content of the utterances" (Bruce, 1977, 255). New denominations of Christian-Believers have come into existence due to this issue of "tongues."

In 1906, in the Azusa Street Mission of Los Angeles, "the fire was lit," and gifts were in motion once again. By 1914, the director of a Pentecostal Church publicly called for a great gathering of Christian-Believers in the baptism of the Holy Spirit, and out of that gathering emerged the Assemblies of GOD, the main Pentecostal denomination in the United States (Gonzalez, 1985, 255). The founder of the Assemblies of GOD was Charles Mason (Noll, 1992, 494). It is the belief of the Assemblies of GOD that tongues are the manifestations of the Holy Spirit just like on the Day of Pentecost. The development and sustainment of a new denomination just reiterates the importance of the operating of the Holy Spirit gifts for the twenty-first century Christian-Believers. Remember **Luke 12:48** *But he that knew not, and did commit things worthy of stripes, shall be beaten with few stripes. For unto whomsoever much is given, of him shall be much required: and to whom men have committed much, of him they will ask the more.*

The Holy Spirit and HIS Gifts are an essential part of the Christian-Believer's faith and development of the Church. Spiritual gifts are from GOD, given by GOD through the power and direction of the Holy Spirit. The Spirit is here to comfort and to assist Christian-Believers to fulfill their calling of the Great Commission. It is important for Christian-Believers to let the world know that GOD is not gone or dead; HE is alive. HE gives us a comforter until Jesus Christ's return.

The Fruit of the Holy Spirit

Galatians 5:22–23 *But the fruit of the Spirit is love, joy, peace, longsuffering, gentleness, goodness, faith,* *[23]MEEKNESS, temperance: against such there is no law."*

The Apostle Paul writes concerning the fruit of the Spirit that all Christian-Believers should obtain and retain in their lives accordingly. These items, although individually named, are all part of one fruit in the Spirit. They all require the denying of self and the crucifying of flesh. Having the fruit of the Spirit is perpendicular to Western culture, which promotes individualism and independence. To Eastern culture, it is antagonistic because it requires implementation of the fruit of the Spirit to all persons regardless of ethnicity, class, and/or family name.

The indwelling of the Holy Spirit requires giving fruit to your enemies. Manifestation of the fruit of the Spirit represents commitment of the Christian-Believer to the GODhead. When the Christian-Believer disciplines their mind, body, and spirit to align with GOD's WORD, it causes them to produce the items listed in the fruit of the Spirit. "Disciplines are activities of mind and body purposefully undertaken to bring our personality and total being into effective cooperation with the divine order" (Willard, 1999, 68). This discipline is available only through continuous behaviors known as habits. Our habits impart conditional learning that affects behavior and lifestyle. The habits of Christian-Believers are transformed by our interaction with GOD (Willard, 1999, 118), which will allow these habits to be imparted into our lifestyle.

The Christian-Believer's lifestyle speaks to the world through the fruit of the Holy Spirit. No matter how many times a person goes to Church, the amount of money given for tithes, and the time spent with layperson ministry, without the manifestation of the fruit it is all void. When Saul tried to validate his disobedience, this was Samuel's response. **1 Samuel 15:22** *And Samuel said, Hath the Lord as great delight in burnt offerings and sacrifices, as in obeying the voice of the Lord? Behold, to obey is better than sacrifice, and to hearken than the fat of rams.*

Faith is something that Christian-Believers must understand. **Hebrews 11:6** *But without faith it is impossible to please GOD.* The fruit of the Spirit is non-negotiable; it resonates through the daily activities of the Christian-Believer's personality and lifestyle choices. Paul writes in **Galatians 5:22** *But the fruit of the Spirit is love, joy, peace, longsuffering, gentleness, goodness, faith,*[23] *Meekness, temperance: against such there is no law..* That means there is no law to validate going against the fruit of the Spirit.

Expectation

Romans 12:6–8 *Having then gifts differing according to the grace that is given to us, whether prophecy, let us prophecy according to the proportion of faith;* [7]*Or ministry, let us wait on*

*our ministering: or he that teacheth, on
teaching; 8) Or he that exhorteth, on
exhortation: he that giveth, let him do
it with simplicity; he that ruleth, with
diligence; he that showeth mercy, with
cheerfulness.*

In these Scriptures, Paul is showing that
the basis for your gift's manifestation is your
faith and willingness to humble yourself to the
authority of Scripture. Billy Graham, a world-
renowned minister of GOD, was struggling at
a point in his ministry to humble himself to
Scripture according to the portion of his faith.
"But in an act of faith and trust, Billy Graham
decided to trust the totality of GOD's WORD.
He said 'Father, I am going to accept this as Thy
WORD—by faith! I am going to allow faith to go
beyond my intellectual questions and doubts,
and I will believe this to be your inspired WORD.'
Billy Graham believes that his ministry never
would have been blessed by GOD had he not, in
faith, trusted all of the Bible's teachings" (Rainer,
2001, 126). Today, the distinction between
"good" and "evil" is not by righteousness and
unrighteousness but rather between having
and not having (Wells, 1994, 49), which is
perpendicular to the Scripture's teachings.

GOD the Holy Spirit gives us power. The
reason we do not serve in power is that we fail

to walk under the control of the Spirit (Reid, 2002, 44). The Holy Spirit and HIS gifts are what Christian-Believers need to have to fight against the enemy, not a big building and jam fest. "In America, our Churches can have the finest buildings, the best resources, the latest version of Power Point presentation, and praise teams that could win a Grammy award—but without the Spirit, we've got no game" (Reid, 2002, 45).

In America, many people say they are Christians, but they have little idea what that means, much less actually acknowledge Christ as the forgiver and leader of their life (McRaney, 2003, 33). This lack of faith, commitment to Christ, and the authority of Scripture, which is sin, leaves Christian-Believers vulnerable to the attacks of the enemy. "Sin is not just not trusting GOD only by the act of wrongdoing but a state of alienation from GOD" (Elwell, 2001, 1103). **James 1:14** *But every man is tempted, when he is drawn away of his own lust, and enticed.* It is critical for Christian-Believers to realize that nobody is going to be converted or convinced of the truthfulness of biblical or theological issues in question without the work of the Holy Spirit (Hindson & Caner, 2008, 267). The Spirit is something that all Christian-Believers have to fight off the enemy using others and ourselves.

THE LOST SON AND DAUGHTER

Jesus's story of the Lost Son in **Luke 15:11–24** is a definition of lost sons and daughters of GOD and HIS compassion and forgiveness toward a repentant heart. The first error is the use of the word *prodigal* instead of lost. The father did not say that his son was reckless and now is straight but rather that his son was **lost** and now he is "found." Being lost is not a determinant of a behavior; rather, it is an illustration of one's obedience to the WORD of GOD and serving the GODhead. The son in this Scripture did not do anything illegal or immoral but rather had a lavish life away from his father and upbringing. This lavish life occurs today when people leave the GODhead and seek the world for purpose, fulfillment, and sustainment. You may question how that is possible, let me enlighten you. When you can choose an occupation that is contrary to the WORD of GOD, you are lost.

When you think more about watching football, baseball, basketball, and any other sport more than serving GOD's people, you are lost. When your focus for money is to buy cars, clothes, jewelry, houses, etc., instead of building the house of faith (i.e. Church), you are lost. When pleasure in this world is more important than obedience to the GODhead, you are lost. When your family name, ethnicity, family heritage, and economic status are the determinant of who you are to establish yourself, you are lost. If the GODhead acceptance is not at the forefront of your mind when you made any decision concerning your life or the influence you have over others, you are lost.

Overt sins are obvious and easily identifiable, but that does not make covert sins any less significant toward the downfall of GOD's creation. A misinterpretation of the parable is that a lost person is obstinate, a drunkard, an adulterer, and mischievous. It is not difficult to miss an alternative interpretation that states what the lost son did was evil not because of the overt sins. This lost son could have done evil by not attending worship service, paying tithes, giving the needy, etc. Being lost is not constrained to the obvious disobedience of the Ten Commandments but rather the consistency of rebellion against the WORD of GOD. A covert sin includes not praying daily but rather only in severe scenarios. Paul wrote in **Romans 7:19** *The good that I would do I do not and the evil I should not do that is what I find myself doing,* in addition **1 Corinthians 15:30** Paul writes, *"I die daily."*

Paul understands that where the law is, evil is present. The enemy will try to convince Christian-Believers to turn away from GOD the Father, Jesus Christ the Son, GOD the Holy Spirit, and if they listen, they too are in the group of the lost son and daughter. Many times, Christian-Believers think the blessings of GOD are individualistic, focusing on the recipient rather than the body of Christ. Believing the gifts and callings of GOD are discretionary and dependent upon the person apart from GOD is ridiculous. Exercising the spiritual gifts is not without responsibility and accountability to the GODhead or the Church. This ideology is why many Christian-Believers are in the lost son and daughter group.

Nothing that GOD gives us is just for us as an individual. When we look at Scripture, Sampson's strength was not for sport or exaltation of himself but rather as a protector of GOD's people. Many times, Christian-Believers are lost because their behavior is one of ritualistic behavior that does not correspond with the Spirit or movement of the Church. People forget who gave them the Gifts and who is the author and finisher of the faith.

Paul writes in **Romans 1:25** *Who changed the truth of GOD into a lie, and worshipped and served the creature more than the creator.* Christian-Believers do this when they esteem people more than they esteem GOD. An example of this esteem is when people get excited when particular people are preaching but do not get excited in that way at their local Church, paying tithes, giving offering, or when being called by the Holy Spirit to do foreign evangelism. Getting the motivation from a Christian-Believer's conference or revival is not the focus of this discussion because anyone can get excited in a vibrant environment. I want to see Christian-Believers get excited serving GOD and HIS people. The focus is your behavior at your local home Church with the pastor, leadership, and ministry events.

Do you think GOD wanted to see people in bondage, slavery, or segregation? Do racism and sexism depict righteous attributes of Christian-Believers? Words like *ethnocentricity, individualism, egocentrism*, etc. describe behavior types of lost people. An example of the lost son occurs when a person focuses more on their societal acceptance, national heritage, physique, tangible objects, DNA, and pigmentation rather than their relationship with Jesus Christ and the promises GOD has for them. If you were to have a conversation with Jesus Christ right now, would the discussion be about race, ethnicity, culture, natural heritage, family lineage, sexism, etc.? Would it be fair for Jesus Christ to proportion HIS attention based upon those lost persons' ideologies? GOD does not like these types of behaviors, nor do the righteous men and women of GOD exhibit such behaviors. Being righteous is not easy and requires a lot. **1 Peter 4:18** *And if the righteous scarcely be saved, where shall the ungodly and the sinner appear?*

I am so glad Christ loves me and listens to my prayer just because I am Christian-Believer—nothing more, nothing less. The Christian-Believer esteems their relationship with Jesus Christ and their obedience to the WORD of GOD above all else (nationalism, family heritage, etc.). The WORD of GOD is the premise for life and decision-making for Christian-Believers. It is not what family members recite, traditions of ancestors, or what people of a particular geographic location do that makes the decision but rather what is written in Scripture. Jesus Christ is coming back for a Church without spot or blemish, not people from a specific geographic location, culture, denomination, or a particular DNA. GOD cares about obedience to the WORD of GOD; HE is not concerned about temporal things (i.e. money, assets, family, social status, or nationality) that have no effect on His eternal plans.

- Will being born in Honduras, England, or Thailand provide salvation through Jesus Christ? NO.
- Does your culture, chromosomes, or genetics provide a Spiritual anointing

from GODhead? NO.
- Will your IQ motivate the Holy Spirit to give you a particular or Calling or Gift? NO.
- Is pigmentation a motive that will persuade the GODhead to secure your pathway to Heaven? NO.
- Can a PhD give you more grace from the GODhead than a third-grade education? NO.

Lost people do not know the vernacular of the Scriptures concerning Righteous people and Saints of GOD.

Righteous People

They think righteous people are a select group of people who are hypocrites or ordained by a religious authority. Both ideas are outside the Biblical definition of faith in the GODhead. This insufficiency represents why righteous or righteousness is a term of great excitement used in movies rather than representing a holy and blameless Christina-Believer's lifestyle. It is written in **Romans 4:20, 22** that Abraham's faith was counted unto him as righteousness. The term righteous means a lifestyle of Faith N Motion and wearing the righteousness of the GODhead, not your own, given unto you by Jesus Christ. Christian-Believers ought to be called righteous just like Noah, Abraham, and Job.,

Do not confuse **Romans 3:10** as a conflict with **Romans 4:20, 22** because the content and context are different. Romans 3:10 is talking about the Jews' thought of "righteousness" of themselves apart from the GODhead that gives them an advantage over Gentiles. **Romans 3:1,** asks the question, *What advantage then hath the Jew? Or what profit is there of circumcision?* The Jews thought their righteousness a result of their heritage, ethnicity, and culture (i.e. Abraham, Israel, David, etc.) apart from the Godhead, but it was not.

Righteousness is given from the GODhead to Christian-Believers with unwavering faith and commitment to serve the GODhead. The description of righteousness is found in **Psalms 37:30–31** *The mouth of the righteous speaketh wisdom, and his tongue talketh of judgment. 31 The law of his GOD is in his heart; none of his steps shall slide.* Paul reiterates this commitment of faith to obtain righteousness in **Romans 4:16** *Therefore it is of faith, that it might be by grace; to the end the promise might be sure to all the seed; not to that only which is of the law, but to that also which is of the faith of Abraham; who is the father of us all.*

Hebrews 11:6 says, *But without faith it is impossible to please HIM: for he that cometh to GOD must believe that HE is, and that HE is a* *rewarder of them that diligently seek HIM.* The benefits of being a righteous person comes from **James 5:16** *Confess your faults one to another, and pray one for another, that ye may be healed. The effectual fervent prayer of a righteous man availeth much.* Peter the Apostle declares the importance and benefits of being in a righteous position before the Lord. **1 Peter 4:18** *And if the righteous scarcely be saved, where shall the ungodly and the sinner appear?* The righteous will barely make it in.

Saints of GOD

Have you ever heard or sung the song, "*Oh when the Saints go marching in, oh when the Saints go marching in, oh how I want to be in that NUMBER when the Saints go marking in?*" Who are saints of GOD from a Biblical perspective? In the Bible, saints are people of the GODhead who have implemented love the Lord *"with all thy heart, with all thy mind, and with all thy might"* (**Matthew 22:37**). Today's society ridicules persons by calling them a saint; the name is not used as a compliment for righteous behavior but rather as an insult for ridicule.

This jesting can come when a Christian-Believer tries to give advice to another Christian-Believer and the person says, "Who do you think you are, you are not a saint." This comment is decidedly perpendicular to Scripture. Christian-Believers are saints of GOD; if they are not, then the blessings of the New Testament are not for them. GOD the Spirit intercedes for the saints of GOD – **Romans 8:27** *And he that searcheth the hearts knoweth what is the mind of the Spirit, because he maketh intercession for the saints according to the will of GOD).* The five-fold ministry is for the perfecting of the saints of GOD – **Ephesians 4:11–12** *And HE gave some, apostles; and some, prophets; and some, evangelists; and some, pastors and teachers;* [12] *For the **perfecting of the saints**, for the work of the ministry, for the edifying of the body of Christ.*

Saints are not perfect but striving for perfection according to the will of the GODhead. The saints of GOD will judge the world. **1 Corinthians 6:2** *Do ye not know that the saints shall judge the world? And if the world shall be judged by you, are ye unworthy to judge the smallest matters?* Lastly, the saints are the ones going to Heaven. The saints of GOD will be taken to Heaven. **Daniel 7:18** *But the saints of the most High shall take the kingdom, and possess the kingdom for ever, even for ever and ever.* Being a saint is necessary for salvation.

Diversity

Lost people focus on who they are (i.e. ethnicity, nationality, sex, gender, etc.) not on *whose* they are (i.e. children of the GODhead), what they have (i.e. money, houses, cars, etc.) not what they are giving (charity, hope, and longsuffering). Quit playin' with the GODhead, focus on the things that are vertical (i.e. salvation, Heaven, Atonement, righteousness, sainthood, and charity) rather than horizontal (i.e. cars, houses, money, jewelry, entertainment, etc., which are all carnal and pagan.). Do you want GOD to start placing judgment or blessing on you because of your culture, ethnicity, or nationality? Where would you be located if there were categorization requirements on salvation, blessing, atonement, remission of sin, grace, mercy, callings, and gifts from GOD? What if GOD said only the people who are of the straight lineage from Abraham, Isaac, Jacob, Judah, David, Solomon, and Joseph the husband of Mary are permitted to Speak in Tongues, receive the Callings of the Holy Spirit, operate in the Gifts of the Holy Spirit, and be leaders in the Church, where would your ministry fit in?

What will happen if GOD made discriminations concerning your prayers to HIM? What if HE only allowed prayer on Wednesdays and Saturdays from females who are not Holy Ghost-filled with the evidence of Speak in Tongues? How would you feel if you were a female? Can you determine your sex, no because it is your deoxyribonucleic acid (DNA). This is why GOD does not like discriminate on things we are BORN with (i.e. myelination, sex, heritage, hair color, eye color, etc.) but rather our heart toward serving HIM through obedience, meekness, and a contrite spirit. Would you want GOD to discriminate or have prejudice against you based upon ethnicity, sex, or race? Why then do you discriminate against HIS people in worship services (i.e. ethnicity or culture-focused churches) or with hospitality? **Galatians 3:28** *There is neither Jew or Greek, bond or free, there is neither male or female for ye are all one in Christ Jesus.*

Is not the creation of diverse languages that propagated into diverse cultures, which now illuminates diverse ethnicities, a punishment from GOD for humans arrogance and disobedience of servitude with trying to build the Tower of Babel (**Genesis 11:7**)? It is the inability of people to comprehend that everyone is descendants of two people (i.e. Adam and Eve) and we are all from the same Creator. Diversity has led to wars, genocide, prejudice, discrimination, and stereotypes because we do not love one another as Christ loved us (**John**

13:34). Do you think on Judgement Day GOD will take into consideration your sex, education, financial status, culture, and ethnicity? No, those things are not what GOD esteems; rather, it is faith. **Hebrews 10:38** *Now the just shall live by faith: but if any man draw back, my soul shall have no pleasure in HIM.* **Hebrews 11:6** *But without faith it is impossible to please GOD for he that cometh to God must believe that he is, and that he is a rewarder of them that diligently seek HIM.* The one language is coming back for GOD's people, according to **Zephaniah 3:9** *For then will I turn to the people a **pure language**, that they may **all** call upon the name of the Lord, to serve HIM **with one consent**.*

Part V
Christian-Believer Attributes

Proverbs 23:7
For As He Thinketh In His Heart, So Is He: Eat And Drink, Saith He To Thee; But His Heart Is Not With Thee.

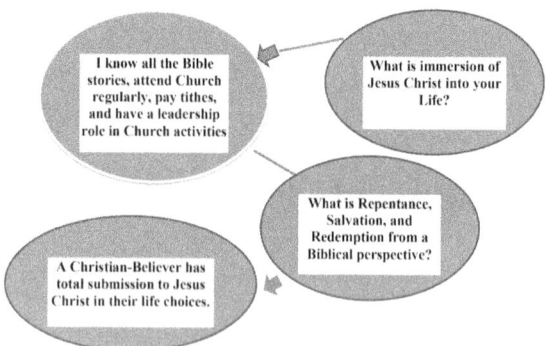

MARKS OF MATURITY

Determination of maturity in the Christ Jesus is not by age, membership, or residence at a Church. It is determined by our personal relationship, obedience, and commitment with Jesus Christ, which is evident by our spiritual growth. If a person continues to live in the same life and with the same life choices before meeting Christ and afterward, they are not of the faith nor are they Christian-Believers but religious. Christianity requires growth in order to be the person GOD has called you to be. **John 3:16** meant one thing to me when I was young; however, as I have grown, my understanding of that Scripture has also grown. When I was young, I understood that GOD loves me and is always there for me. Where I am now, I understand that the love of GOD permeates all areas of prejudice, stereotypes, and societal class structures to identify me as one of HIS children, and that love establishes me as one of the peculiar people of Jesus Christ with an inheritance of Abraham, Isaac, Israel, Moses, and the Saints of GOD.

Christian-Believers can become complacent and stagnant in their walk with the GODhead. The Apostle Paul speaks about Christian-Believers caught up in religion. These persons do not grow because they yield not to the Spirit that operates through faith, which offers freedom and liberty. 2

Corinthians 3:17 *Now the Lord is that Spirit: and where the Spirit of the Lord is there is liberty.* Jesus Christ came to set us free because when you are free you are free in deed.

Matthew 11:28 *Come unto me, all ye that labour and are heavy laden, and I will give you rest.* It can be interpreted that **Matthew 11:28** means "come as you are." Christ does not say come as you are; rather, HE says come and HE will give you rest. Jesus invites all to come to HIM and HIS way. HE will accept a person when they come with a penitent heart; however, a person is not to remain in their current fleshly, carnal, and pagan state. Instead, they are to grow in the Spirit of GOD.

The Apostle John gives his new converts a Scripture to assist in their understanding that their walk with Christ is a journey not a position, and the journey is sanctification not stagnation. Christian-Believers must continue to develop their spiritual foundation, which is exemplified in their lifestyle choices. As their understanding of GOD's WORD grows, so will their connection with the Holy Spirit. **III John 1:2** *Beloved, I wish above all things that thou mayest prosper and be in health, even as thy soul prospereth.* The soul cannot prosper if the spiritual person does not prosper in the Holy Spirit.

THE ELECT

In **Colossians 3:5-16,** Paul writes to the new
converts concerning their spiritual formation
and their title as being "the elect." The elect
were not like the common persons; rather, they
were chosen and set apart for GOD's service.
Paul was familiar with this elect class because he
was also part of the tribe of Benjamin. It is the
tribe of Benjamin stayed with Judah during the
separation (**1 Kings 12:21**) in the book of Kings.
Benjamin respected GOD's ordinance that the
kingship of Israel would remain in the household
of David and stayed with the tribe of Judah (**2
Samuel 7:16**). The children of Israel, GOD's Elect,
were at a mountain with Moses. The children of
Israel were to be priests to the nations and GOD's
representatives on earth.

Paul gives the Colossians a bit of **Galatians
5** with a twist. Paul outlines attributes associated
with the elect class by giving examples.
Colossians 3:13 *Forbearing one another, and
forgiving one another, if any man have a quarrel
against any: even as Christ forgave you, so also do
ye.* Paul is giving the Colossians the other side of
being a Christian-Believer, the responsibilities.
Walking in brotherly love no matter the offense
means denying self. You can only walk in this
denial of self when you communicate with GOD
and develop your spiritual foundation.

As new creatures in Christ and part of the elect, Paul instructs the Colossians to have such a mentality and attitude toward others. As Christian-Believers, we walk in this newness of mind with mercy, kindness, meekness, humbleness, longsuffering, and charity. There would be a manifestation of their spiritual foundation development. This manifestation represented their maturity in the spirit. Being the elect measurement is not by the amount of time. Elect status is not determined by the amount of tithes you pay at Church or to charitable organizations. The elects are Christian-Believers who have Faith N Motion and operate in the GODhead callings, manifestation of the gifts, with the workings from fruit of the Spirit, and the ability to walk in charity no matter the environment. Ethnicity, economic status, geography is of no consequence because you are serving of GOD through being a servant to HIS people (**Matthew 23:11**). When you are part of the elect, the focus is on where you are going (i.e. Heaven to be with the GOD) and not where you come from or your DNA. The only source that concerns you about acceptance is the GODhead.

The calling is the five-fold ministry given by GOD the Holy Spirit to Christian-Believers— apostle, prophet, evangelist, pastor, teacher

(**Ephesians 4:11**). Preachers, deacons, and elders are not part of the five-fold ministry, but rather they are helpers to the ministry. A preacher is the noun of the action word to preach. A deacon was first used to feed the widows because the apostles stated in **Acts 6:2** *It is not reason that we should leave the WORD of GOD, and serve tables.* The gifts are the nine manifestations of GOD the Holy Spirit through Christian-Believers—word of wisdom, word of knowledge, faith, gifts of healing, working of miracles, prophecy, discerning of spirits, diverse tongues, and interpretation of tongues (**1 Corinthians 12:8–10**). The fruit are made up of nine attributes given by GOD the Holy Spirit for Christian-Believers to emulate— love, joy, peace, long-suffering, gentleness, goodness, faith, meekness, and temperance. The fruit of GOD the Holy Spirit reinforce the calling and gifts in an overt expression for other Christian-Believers, Christlike persons, Believers, and Unbelievers. The calling, gifts, and fruit of GOD the Spirit reinforce GOD on earth through exhibition from Christian-Believers.

As we discipline ourselves in our activities for GOD, spiritual maturity takes place, and obtaining the elect status is possible. Peter, one of four of the elect apostles, writes in **1 Peter 4:18** *And if the righteous scarcely be saved,*

where shall the ungodly and the sinner appear?
Only GOD can help change our thoughts that
mold our actions that create a personality that
exhibits habits.

Our thoughts create who we are because
what we think about most often reflects our
values, morals, and sense of reasoning. We
invest in our thoughts through resources
such as money, time, intellectual activity, and
brain space. If we think more about worldly
possessions, then that is where our actions
will form. When we think about our servitude
to the GODhead, then our actions will exhibit
such revelations. As our thoughts lean toward
the GODhead, so will our actions. Instead of
entertaining ourselves with television shows,
video games, sports, cooking, hunting, and
eating, we spend those times on reading the
Bible, studying the content and context of
Scripture, and memorizing the WORD of GOD
through reciting Scripture by book, chapter,
and verse. Many people can quote a Scripture
to include Satan, but how many can quote the
book, the chapter, and verse without the Bible
being available?

Actions can either allow you to
communicate with people with a benefit that
lasts for only a season or allow you to help save
someone's life for eternity, like your own life.

Actions will change our personality. A change in personality changes our lifestyle. As our lifestyle changes, it will affect a cultural change. Yes, if you want to see a change in your family, friends, neighborhood, city, county, state, country and world, start by first changing your thoughts, actions, personality, lifestyle, and habits. It is at the lifestyle choices where the manifestation of the Elect Christian-Believer resonates and flourishes. The lifestyle shows what you do at work, at home, and at Church. The lifestyle is not a "show" but rather a way of living. The continuous operation in a particular lifestyle becomes a habit. For instance, the more you exercise and eat healthy food, the more you will *want* to exercise and eat healthy food. When the gifts and the fruit of GOD the Holy Spirit are part of your lifestyle, operating in the gifts and fruit becomes a habit.

CHURCH MEMBERSHIP

Motivation can take on two characteristics for a person: intrinsic and extrinsic. The intrinsic is internal to the individual. This type of motivation places all the responsibility on the person. It is the individual's responsibility to want to learn, and it is within this area that they will want to learn because of self-motivation. Extrinsic represents the opposite of intrinsic. Extrinsic places the responsibility of learning on someone else. Both approaches have positive and negative connotations.

Intrinsic motivation can have a false sense of reality when it comes to serving GOD. For instance, many new converts believe when they come to Jesus that all their problems will go away. They assume that following Christ will make all their current situations disappear. This assumption is false. Jesus promises love and salvation not immunity from life's struggles. Jesus says that He is the way and the light, and no one comes to the Father expect by Him. Jesus does not promise a life of no struggles or problems.

Extrinsic factors cause many people to leave the Church. The external influence that produces motivation is the predictor of the person's action. For instance, many people in the "faith" that supposedly represented GOD have done things apart from Scripture. The motivation behind these peoples' dedication to GOD was through a human not divine inspiration. Many "leaders" of GOD have caused many Christian-Believers to stray from the truth because their ideologies and teaching were pseudo (i.e. false) without a solid biblical basis.

Pseudo-Bibles do not count. If the persons writing a bible are not Christian-Believers with a solid foundation in the theology and spirit of the WORD, then their doctrine about GOD is written in a pseudo-book. People who serve GOD through something external and not internal walk away from GOD because of a disagreement over superficial ideologies (i.e. color of the carpet) are not Christian-Believers but those who *fell by the wayside, on stony ground, or on thorns* (**Luke 8: 5-7**). Unless the GODhead tells you to leave a Church, you stay put. It is a common occurrence for people to hop churches because they feel as though GOD is calling them to open their own Church. The devil is a liar; GOD does not come to destroy or separate the body of Christ but to fulfil and unite. Remember that GOD had Hosea to marry a harlot on purpose (**Hosea 1:2**).

Richards and Bredfeldt, from the book *Creative Bible Teaching,* postulate that a "teacher-student relationship can be cultivated or destroyed by the teacher's attitude in class" (1998, 232). This ideology supports the motivation of extrinsic faith. If the determinant of motivation is a result of something external to the student, then that is not motivation but excitement. A person motivates himself or herself while outsiders entertain or excite us. Group dynamics also places the teacher and students on par with each other. "It is dangerous to equate the words *teacher* and *authority*.

An authority is, by definition, a person with the power to settle issues, the right (even duty) to control, command, and determine. And each of these activities is destructive to student motivation, a denial of the teacher's true role" (Richards & Bredfeldt, 1998, 232). This perspective is why many people attend Church and lack the full understanding of the gospel. When Paul taught the Galatians, Ephesians, or the Colossians, the lessons were not up for debate or discussion. The teaching came with authority and was for knowledge of GOD, not pleasing of men. Any person whom GOD calls to the ministry, HE also equips (**Exodus 3:10–12**).

Structural factors are more culture-based than factual. In the United States, where individualism is preferred, people learn best when the teaching "has an overall plan to learning that provides a pattern, logical sequence, and encouraged" (Richards & Bredfeldt, 1998, 237). People place value on results. This practice is normal for cultures that have a stable environment where physical needs, such as medical and dietary needs, are met. In countries were community and family are important, learning is for the benefit of the people. In some African countries, teaching is to support the family traditions and cultural cohesiveness and provide immediate solutions to problems. These people are not concerned about what tomorrow brings but rather how they live today.

The motivation of Church members to learn is not the responsibility of the Church. A teacher, who is called by GOD, has the responsibility to ensure that proper understanding of the Scripture is taught to the body. The teacher has the responsibility from GOD and accountability to GOD. **Hebrews 13:21** *Obey them that have rule over you, and submit yourselves; for they watch for your souls, as they must give account, that they may do it with joy, and not with grief.* It is an individual responsibility to cultivate motivation through their relationship with GOD, *for it is GOD which worketh in you both to will and to do of HIS good pleasure* (**Phil 2:13**).

When motivation for the individual is by any outside source apart from GOD, that motivation will fail. This is evident throughout biblical Scriptures. Men and women of GOD, who are called by GOD, must develop their relationship with GOD apart from outside sources or internal preference. Examples include Moses at Mount Sinai, Jeremiah with the children of Israel, Jesus with the disciples, and Paul with the Gentiles. The WORD of GOD was their motivation without any presentation. These men knew GOD personally, and this was enough. When the presentation determines the motivation to learn the WORD of GOD, then those people do not want to know GOD's WORD. The WORD of GOD is enough for Christian-Believers who truly love GOD and want to serve HIM, and for those in which it is not, they are **PLAYIN A GAME AND DON'T KNOW THE RULES: The Reality of Christianity.**

REALITY OF CHRISTIANITY

SYNOPSIS OF THE MATTER

Christian-Believers of the past died for the WORD of GOD. The Roman Emperor Nero tortured Christian-Believers as entertainment for the crowd before killing them. This Roman would put fur on them to attract dogs, some were crucified, and others were set on fire to illuminate the night (Gonzalez, 1984, 35). Anyone can be Christlike or a Believer by reciting a definition of terms, but only a select few can be a Christian-Believer. Being a Christian-Believer requires accepting the Bible at its core of understanding with comprehension in the content and context Scripture. The Christian-Believer enjoys the blessing and chastisements of the Lord because they know the Lord *chasteneth those whom he loves* (**Hebrews 12:6**). In perspective, the GODhead loves you. Do not allow words such as "chasteneth" to confuse you. If disobedience of the GODhead had not been part of life on earth with a derivative consequence of Hellfire, then acceptance and blessing of the GODhead has no merit. Accepting the Bible as the source of learning and understanding GOD the Father, GOD the Son, and GOD the Holy Spirit is necessary to establish a foundation in Christianity in order to become a Christian-Believer.

Secondly, Christian-Believers must accept the whole Bible as the sole authority in which all behavior is measured. If we cannot agree on these concepts, there will not be a Christian or Biblical conversation. Christian-Believers' values and convictions cannot originate through intelligence, academia, deductive reasoning, inductive reasoning, or society influence. The premise for believing must be faith-based, internally charged with internal and external life application behavior and attributes.

Christian-Believers walk in faith with the GODhead, which is GOD the Father (i.e. the Creator), Jesus Christ (i.e. GOD the Son, savior of the whole world, remitter and forgiver of all sins), and GOD the Holy Spirit (i.e. The Spirit of GOD, baptism of the Holy Ghost, imparter of callings, spiritual gifts, and fruit of the Holy Spirit). The GODhead assures the Christian-Believer that they are able to provide protection against any foe; give guidance on past, present, or future events; and secure salvation with a resting place in Heaven. If a person does not believe in the GODhead and does not accept the WHOLE Bible's established commandments, principles, and ideologies as inspired by the GODhead, then the principles that establish Biblical truth are invalid. The absence of such distinctions concerning the five-fold ministry, spiritual gifts, spiritual callings, Heaven and Hell are literal places represents that there can be no theological discussion on the definition of these subjects.

Distinctions concerning the GODhead, personal relationship, audible and visual manifestations of Heavenly creatures (ANGELs), the five-fold ministry (apostle, prophet, evangelist, pastor, teacher), nine gifts of the Spirit (word of wisdom, word of knowledge, faith, gift of healings, working miracles, prophecy, discernment of spirits, interpretation of tongues, and diverse tongues), and Heaven and Hell as literal places are attributes of Christianity that distinguishes this religion from the rest. These attributes separate Christian-Believers from all other participants of other religions. Christianity is a multidimensional religion because GOD is omnipotent, omnipresent, and omniscient. GOD is not limited to time, space, physics, chemistry, biology, technology, and any other ology that shows up. GOD can be in Cairo, Egypt; London, England; Augusta, Georgia (United States); Rio de Janeiro, Brazil; Beijing, China; Lagos, Nigeria; and Seoul, South Korea.

When we discus Christianity we must define the parameters. There can be no theological discussion without clearly defined definitions on subjects. Talking about Christianity builds up our faith. **Romans 10:17** *So then faith cometh by hearing, and hearing by the WORD of GOD.* Conversations about the GODhead build up our faith and prepare Christian-Believers for spiritual awakening and anointing from the GODhead. When the awakening and anointing comes from GOD, so does the calling, gifts, and fruit. Either all the teachings of the Bible are ALL true, or none of them are true. Do not let your limitation of discernment prevent you from receiving the fullness of GOD's WORD. There are Scriptures I am still learning, and others for which I have to pray for wisdom, but I do not negate their significance because of my ignorance. Be strong and of courage and become a Christian-Believer and stop **PLAYIN A GAME AND DON'T KNOW THE RULES: The Reality of Christianity.**

REFERENCES

1. **Some portion of this material by**
    Britannica Encyclopedia. 2019. *Kings James Version: Sacred Text*. Editors of Encyclopedia Britannica. Retrieved from https://www.britannica.com/topic/King-James-Version /

2. **Some portion of this material by** Bynum, Juanita. 1999. *The Limp of the Lord*. Tulsa, OK, USA: Azusa 1999: Higher Dimensions Evangelistic Center, VHS.

3. **Some portion of this material by**
    Dominy, Bert. 2010. Paul and Spiritual Gifts: Reflections on I Corinthians 12–14. Southwestern Journal of Theology 26, no. 1: 49-68. *ATLA Religion Database with ATLASerials, EBSCOhost.*

4. **Some portion of this material by** Bruce, F.F. 1977. *Paul: Apostle of the Hearts Set Free*. Grand Rapids, MI, USA: William B. Eerdmans.

5. **Some portion of this material by** Carson, D.A, and Douglas J. Moo. 2005. *An Introduction to the New Testament,* 2nd Edition. Grand Rapids, MI, USA: Zondervan.

6. **Some portion of this material by** Duggan, Fr. Michael. 1985. The Cross and the Holy Spirit in Paul: Implications for Baptism in the Holy Spirit. Journal of the Society for

Pentecost Studies. *ATLA Religion Database with ATLASerials, EBSCOhost.*

7. **Some portion of this material by** Elwell, Walter A. 2001. *Evangelical Dictionary of Theology,* 2nd Edition. Grand Rapids, MI, USA: Baker Academic.

8. **Some portion of this material by** Erickson, Millard J. (1998). *Christian Theology*, 2nd ed. Grand Rapids, MI: Baker Academic.

9. **Some portion of this material by** Gonzalez, Justo L. 1984. *The Story of Christianity Volume 1: The Early Church to the Dawn of the Reformation.* New York, NY, USA: HarperCollins.

10. **Some portion of this material by** Gonzalez, Justo L. 1985. *The Story of Christianity Volume 2: The Reformation to the Present Day.* New York, NY, USA: HarperCollins.

11. **Some portion of this material by** Hamburger, R. B. T., under Versöhnung und Versöhnungstag; Zunz, S. P. pp. 76-80; Sachs, Die Religiöse Poesic der Juden in Spanien, 1845, pp. 172 et seq.; Brueck, Pharisäische Volkssitten, 1855, pp. 135–146.K.

12. **Some portion of this material by** Hindson, Ed, and Ergun Caner. 2008. *The Popular Encyclopedia of Apologetics.* Eugene, IN, USA: Harvest House.

13. **Some portion of this material by** Jameison, Robert, A.R. Fausset, and David Brown. 1961. *Jameison, Fausset, and Brown's Commentary.* Grand Rapids, MI, USA: Zondervan.

14. **Some portion of this material by** LaSor, William S., David Allan Hubbard, and Frederic William Bush. 1982, 1996. *The Message, Form, and Background of the Old Testament: Old Testament Survey,* 2nd Edition. Grand Rapids, MI, USA: Eerdmans Publishing.

15. **Some portion of this material by** Lea, Thomas D., and David Alan Black. 2003. *The New Testament: Its Background and Message,* 2nd Edition. Nashville, TN, USA: Broadman & Holman.

16. **Some portion of this material by** MacArthur, John F. Jr. 1982. The Mandate of Biblical Inerrancy: Expository Preaching. *ATLASerial: American Theological Library Association.*

17. **Some portion of this material by** McDowell, Josh, and Don Stewart. 1983. *The Handbook of Today's Religions.* Nashville, TN, USA: Thomas Nelson.

18. **Some portion of this material by** McRaney, Will Jr. 2003. *The Art of Personal Evangelism.* Nashville, TN, USA: Broadman & Holman.

19. **Some portion of this material by** Morrison, Hector. 2007. The Ascension

of Jesus and the Gift of the Holy Spirit. *ATLA Religion Database with ATLASerials, EBSCOhost.*

20. **Some portion of this material by** Noll, Mark A. 1992. *A History of Christianity in the United States and Canada.* Grand Rapids, MI, USA: William B. Eerdmans.

21. **Some portion of this material by** Parsons, George W. 1981. The Structure and Purpose of the Book of Job. *Bibliotheca Sacra, BSC* 138:55.

22. **Some portion of this material by** Pipes, Jerry, and Victor Lee. 1999. *Family to Family: Leaving a Lasting Legacy.* Alpharetta, GA, USA: North American Mission Board.

23. **Some portion of this material by** Price, Terry. 2007. *Gird Up Your Loins.* Maranatha Baptist Bible College. Waltertown, WI, USA. (Fall/Winter).

24. **Some portion of this material by** Rainer, Thom S. 2001. *Surprising Insights from the UnChurched and Proven Ways to Reach Them.* Grand Rapids, MI, USA: Zondervan

25. **Some portion of this material by** Rainer, Thom S. 2005. *The Unexpected Journey: Conversations with People Who Turned from Other Beliefs to Jesus.* Grand Rapids, MI, USA: Zondervan.

26. **Some portion of this material by** Reid, Alvin L. 2002. *Radically UnChurched: Who*

They Are & How to Reach Them. Grand Rapids, MI, USA: Kregel Publications.

27. **Some portion of this material by** Richards, Lawrence, and Gary Bredfeldt. 1998. *Creative Bible Teaching,* Revised and Expanded. Chicago, IL, USA: Moody Publishers.

28. **Some portion of this material by** Shelley, John C. 1992. Job 42:1-6: GOD 's Bet and Job's Repentance. *Review and Expositor, REVEXP* 089:4 (Fall). https://doi.

29. **Some portion of this material by** Thompson, Michael. 2006. The Enigma of Job Focusing on Job 1 and 2. *Chafer Theological Journal,* CJSJ 12.1 (Spring)

30. **Some portion of this material by** Towns, Elmer. 2001. *Theology for Today.* Fort Worth, TX, USA: Harcourt Publishers.

31. **Some portion of this material by** Waters, Larry J. 1997. Reflections on the Suffering from the Book of Job. *Bibliotheca Sacra, BSAC* 154:616.

32. **Some portion of this material by** Wells, David F. 1994. GOD *in the Wasteland: The Reality of Truth in a World of Fading Dreams.* Grand Rapids, MI, USA: William B. Eerdmans.

33. **Some portion of the material by** Willard, Dallas. 1999. *The Spirit of the Disciplines: Understanding How* GOD *Changes Lives.* New York, NY, USA: HarperOne.